People Power

*This limited and signed first edition is issued on
the occasion of Brian O'Connell's retirement
as President of INDEPENDENT SECTOR
Fall 1994*

Brian O'Connell

People Power

Service, Advocacy, Empowerment

*Selected Writings of
Brian O'Connell*

Limited First Edition
The Foundation Center

Copyright © 1994 by Brian O'Connell.
All rights reserved.

Printed and bound in the United States of America.

Library of Congress Cataloging-in-Publication Data
O'Connell, Brian, 1930–
  People Power : service, advocacy, empowerment : selected writings of Brian O'Connell. — Limited 1st ed.
      p.   cm.
  Includes bibliographical references and index.
  ISBN 0-87954-563-1
    1. Voluntarism—United States.   2. Charities—United States.
  3. Nonprofit organizations—United States.   I. Foundation Center.
  II. Title.
  HN90.V64O34   1994
  361.3'7—dc20   94-23368
                                                          CIP

*Dedicated to John W. Gardner
Mentor, Partner, and Friend*

Contents

Foreword xi

1. Origins, Dimensions, and Impact of America's Voluntary Spirit *1*
2. Religion Is Central to the Nonprofit Sector *13*
3. Impact of Nonprofits on Civil Society *17*
4. Philanthropy in Action *23*
5. In Perpetuity or Just for a While? *33*
6. From Service to Advocacy to Empowerment *37*
7. Advocating and Empowering *51*
8. Don't Save Me From the Left or Right *65*
9. What Voluntary Activity Can and Cannot Do for America *67*
10. State of the Sector: With Particular Attention to Its Independence *79*
11. The Relationship Between Voluntary Organizations and Government: Constructive Partnerships/Creative Tensions *93*
12. Community Foundations: More of the Best *107*
13. The Strategic Links Between Business and the Nonprofit Sector *117*
14. Corporate Philanthropy: Getting Bigger, Broader, and Tougher to Manage *123*
15. Guidelines for Giving *133*

16. For Voluntary Organizations in Trouble . . . Or Don't Want to Be   *137*
17. The Role of the Board and Board Members   *153*
18. The Board's Biggest Decision: Hiring the Chief Staff Officer   *165*
19. Compensation in Nonprofit Organizations   *173*
20. The Common Sense of Sabbaticals or Project Leaves   *177*
21. Future Leadership in America   *181*
22. Independence and Interdependence   *187*
23. Investing in Leadership: A Commentary on Applying Common Sense and Proven Models to Resource Development in Nonprofit Organizations   *193*
24. The Growth Fund   *203*
25. The Future Looks Good—For Those Who Invest in It   *215*
26. Citizenship and Community Service: Are They a Concern and Responsibility of Higher Education?   *223*
27. The Meaning of Volunteering   *231*

Index   *235*

Foreword

WHEN THE IDEA was first advanced that I might prepare a book of my writings, I found the notion a bit vain and the merits a bit reaching. When pressed to consider the proposal, I struggled with the fact that I had already published most of these things and the reality that, if they still had value, additional exposure could be useful. I suppose it was the combination of vanity and belief in the ideas that won me over.

At first, the task seemed reasonably easy. All I had to do was assemble a lot of speeches, chapters, testimonies, op-ed pieces and the like; select the best; put them in some order; and ship them off. Oh, how naive I was! The actual experience was the latest of many hard lessons this practitioner has had to learn about the world of writing and publishing. The pieces obviously didn't fit, they were repetitious or contradictory, and they revealed very different styles, or at least different efforts to meet the expectations of varied audiences and publications.

After far more time than I ever thought this project would take, the overall result is still uneven, but I'm reconciled, or perhaps I've rationalized, that a book of writings covering disparate subjects, purposes, and outlets isn't very likely to mesh smoothly.

But having struggled with the myriad parts, I think that what I still want to say comes through, at least well enough to have this second go at it. Also, it seems useful to have in one place certain reference pieces that various people over the years have found instructive, encouraging, or constructively provocative.

At least the Foundation Center thinks so, and I'm grateful for their interest and encouragement. Many of these writings relate to things the Center originally published, and they have been a great source of continuing support and outlet. For this current effort, Sara Engelhardt, Rick Schoff, and Mitch Nauffts of the Center have been patient and prodding, a combination that has helped pull it through. So, too ,with Sharon Stewart and Lisa Wellman at INDEPENDENT SECTOR and with Ann Brown O'Connell.

Helpful funding has been provided by the Prudential Foundation, which awarded me their 1994 Nonprofit Leadership Prize, including $10,000 that I assigned to this project, and by the Durfee Foundation, the George Gund Foundation, the David and Lucile Packard Foundation, and the Premier Industrial Foundation, which have supported a small fund for research, editorial assistance, and other preparation costs for writings on the independent sector as well as for getting the books into the hands of selected national leaders and collections where they might contribute to a better understanding of this side of American life.

Without belaboring my concerns about some disjointedness in the book, a few words of explanation may be useful. There are instances where the same material appears in more than one chapter. I've tried to restrict this to references that seemed necessary to the message at hand. Also, to remove references made irrelevant by the passage of time , to keep the size of the book manageable, and to avoid unnecessary repetition, I've done some considerable excerpting. Where this could cause confusion for someone trying to compare this version with the originals, ellipsis points (. . . .) indicate where material has been left out. Certain chapters, written in different years, contain outdated statistics on giving and volunteering. In one or two instances, there are footnotes referring the reader to chapter 1, which has the most up-to-date figures. For these and any other problems caused by my efforts to adapt these writings to the format of this book, my apologies.

> Brian O'Connell
> Harwich Port, Massachusetts
> July 11, 1994

People Power

Origins, Dimensions, and Impact of America's Voluntary Spirit

INCREASINGLY, WE HEAR THE LAMENT that Americans don't really have a civic spirit anymore. There is a pervasive view that in earlier times we were far more willing than we are today to help one another and to become involved in causes and public issues. It is almost a given that we are now a less caring society and that we should worry about what's happened to all that neighborliness, public spiritedness, and charity.

Actually, the past was not as good as remembered and the present is better than perceived.

A far larger proportion and many more parts of our population are involved in community activity today than at any time in our history. We organize to serve every conceivable aspect of

---

"Origins, Dimensions and Impact of America's Voluntary Spirit," by Brian O'Connell, INDEPENDENT SECTOR, 1986. Revised 1993.

the human condition and are willing to stand up and be counted on almost any public issue. We organize to fight zoning changes, approve bond issues, advocate pro choice or right to life, improve garbage collection, expose overpricing, enforce equal rights, or protest wars. In very recent times we have successfully organized to deal with the rights of women, conservation and preservation, learning disabilities, conflict resolution, Hispanic culture and rights, education on the free enterprise system, the aged, voter registration, the environment, Native Americans, the dying, experimental theater, international understanding, population control, neighborhood empowerment, control of nuclear power, consumerism, and on and on. Volunteers' interests and impact extend from neighborhoods to the ozone layer and beyond.

Approximately 900,000 exempt organizations are officially registered with the Internal Revenue Service, but that does not count religious congregations or the local affiliates of many national organizations such as Boy Scouts and the American Cancer Society. When these and all the less formal neighborhood and community groups are added, the figure is something over two million.

These organizations include the neighborhood improvement societies, Catholic Charities, overseas relief organizations, American Association of Museum Volunteers, private schools and colleges, United Way, corporate foundations and public service programs, United Negro College Fund, fraternal benevolent societies, National Association of Neighborhoods, conservation and preservation groups, Council of Jewish Women, community foundations, National Public Radio, and hundreds of thousands of others. Whether one's interest is wildflowers or civil rights, arthritis or clean air, Oriental art or literacy, the dying or the unborn, organizations are already at work, and if they don't suit one's passion, it is possible to start one's own.

INDEPENDENT SECTOR's 1992 survey, "Giving and Volunteering in the United States," indicated that 51 percent of adults are volunteers, and 14 percent give at least five hours a week to their volunteer assignments. The dollar value of all this contributed time is conservatively estimated at $176 billion.

The base of participation is also spreading. There are more young people, more men, and more older people. Every economic group is involved. There are more people who have problems themselves. The mutual-help movement is the fastest growing side of the voluntary sector. For almost every problem, there is now a group of people who have weathered the storm and are reaching out to help others newly faced with depression, divorce, abuse, or heart surgery.

To the surprise of all who have matter of factly assumed that with so many women now in the workforce it's harder to find female volunteers, the happy reality is that there are more women serving as volunteers. Indeed, several surveys provide the fascinating information that the woman who works for pay is more likely to volunteer than the woman who does not.

One of the reasons so many misconceptions exist about volunteering and nonprofit activity is that this is an aspect of our national life we take for granted and have never really felt a need to study. Now that there seems to be a growing realization that citizen participation is a vital part of our national character, there is greater interest in having a clearer grasp of the facts, trends, and its impact.

Misunderstanding exists on the financial side, as well. Two examples will probably startle all but the most informed reader. Most people assume that foundations and corporations represent a very large proportion of giving in America. As important as their dollars are, the two combined represent only 10 percent of all that is given. Ninety percent comes from individuals.

Furthermore, contributors with incomes under $10,000 contribute about twice as much of their income as do people with incomes of $50,000–$100,000 (3.6 percent compared to 1.7 percent).

IS's survey on giving illustrates that in 1992, 72 percent of all American adults made contributions to the causes of their choice, giving approximately $100 billion, an average of $978 per contributing family.

According to the most recent IS survey, our personal giving breaks down as follows:

      Religion 54.2%
      Education 10.6
      Social Welfare 8.5
      Health & Hospitals 7.8
      Arts & Humanities 7.1

Civic and Public 4.9
Other 7.9

On the volunteering side, the IS survey gives this breakdown:

Religious organizations 17.6%
Informal 15.4
Education 10.1
Youth developments 9.7
Health 8.4
Human services 8.0
Environment 5.6
Work-related organizations 4.6
Recreation—adults 4.4
Public and societal benefit 4.2
Arts, culture, and humanities 4.1
Political organizations 3.1
Other areas of volunteer activity 1.8
International, foreign 1.5
Private and community
    foundations 1.5

In the composite, an almost dizzying array of charitable activity exists. Americans inform, protest, assist, teach, heal, build, advocate, comfort, testify, support, solicit, canvas, demonstrate, guide, feed, criticize, organize, appeal, usher, contribute, and in a hundred other ways serve people and causes.

From where does all this generosity stem? Obviously, ours is not the only participatory society in the world. Giving, volunteering, and nonprofit organizations exist in most countries, but nowhere else are the numbers, proportions, and impact so great.

The comparative studies are sketchy, but what facts there are indicate that this country's degree of organized participation is unique. In a speech entitled "A Global View of Philanthropy," J. D. Livingston Booth of Great Britain, then president of Interphil (International Standing Conference on Philanthropy), said, "Outside the United States there is very little recognition that an independent voluntary sector even exists, let alone that it has a wholeness, a role, and a significance in free societies."

Why is there so much more of this activity here? It's not easy to sort out, but if we hope to sustain it into future generations, we need to understand the phenomenon better than we do. The research and literature are sparse, but one can begin to piece together some of the explanation.

Most often the participation is attributed to our Protestant ethic and English ancestry; but as important as they were, they are only two of many sources. What we identify as Christian, or even Judaeo-Christian impulses, were also brought to our shores by each different wave of immigrants, whether they came from Sweden, Russia, China, or India; and whether they followed Jesus, Moses, Mohammed, or Buddha.

This is not to undervalue the enormous influence of the Puritans and Pilgrims, nor that of English law. One of the most significant writings on the subject comes from John Winthrop, the first governor of Massachusetts. It was a piece he wrote just before he and his fellow Puritans boarded the *Arbella* to come to America in 1630. He read it to them for the first time during the voyage. It is called "A Model of Christian Charity" and was intended to help the group understand how they would have to behave toward one another to survive and make the most of their opportunities in the New World. For example:

> We must be knit together in this work as one man; we must entertain each other in brotherly affection;—we must uphold a familiar commerce together in all meekness, gentleness, patience and liberality. We must delight in each other, make other's conditions our own, rejoice together, mourn together, labor and suffer together; always having before our eyes our commission and community as members of the same body.

One of the largest roles of voluntary organizations concerns religious expression and the protection of that freedom. In the 1993 edition of INDEPENDENT SECTOR's report, "From Belief to Commitment," based on the largest study ever undertaken of the community-service role of religious congregations, extensive documentation shows that religious congregations are the primary service providers for neighborhoods. It is my experience that the poorer the community, the larger that role and impact. Beyond the exercise of religious freedom and the community services provided by religious congregations, these institutions have been and continue to be the places where many moral issues are raised and debated. In his mid-nineteenth-century observations on the American scene, Alexis de Tocqueville saw this country's network of voluntary organizations not so much as service providers but as "the moral associations" where such values as charity and responsibility to others are taught and where the nation's crusades take root.

I am constantly reminded of how much the country's patterns of community service and advocacy relate to the earliest activities of churches and to the initial and continuing protection of freedom of religion. Despite how obvious this is, people tend to set aside this whole half of the voluntary sector as though it does not really belong, relating largely to salvation; but if one looks at what the conscience, the meeting ground, and the organized neighborliness represented by religious congregations mean to the kind of society America is, religion takes on a different and larger significance.

As important as religious influences have been, we can't ascribe our tradition of voluntary action solely to their lessons of goodness. The matter of pure need and mutual dependence and assistance cannot be overlooked. The Minutemen and the frontier families practiced fairly basic forms of enlightened self-interest. To portray our history of volunteering as relating solely to goodness may describe the best of our forebearers, but it ignores the widespread tradition of organized neighborliness that hardship dictated and goodness tempered.

One of the most striking points about our origins is that we shouldn't assume that these characteristics and traditions were imported. In a chapter entitled "Doing Good in the New World," from his book *American Philanthropy*, historian Robert Bremner makes clear that the Indians treated us with far more "Christian" goodness than we practiced on them. Reading his descriptions of the kindly way in which the Indians greeted we intruders and helped us adjust to their world, one is absolutely wrenched out of prior notions about imported goodness.

We came into a country where there was very little structure. We had a chance to start all over again. For most people, for the first time in generations, the family hierarchy was absent. There were few built-in restraints imposed by centuries of laws and habits, and yet we were terribly interdependent. In the absence of extended families and controlling traditions, we addressed our dependence and gregariousness by becoming, as Max Lerner described it, "a nation of joiners." These new institutions, whether they were churches, unions, granges, fire companies, or other specific organizations, became our networks for socializing and mutual activity.

It's also important to realize that we were people determined never again to be ruled by kings or emperors or czars, and thus were suspicious of any central authority. We were resolved that power should be spread. This meant that voluntary institutions carried a large share of what governments did in other countries. In a piece called "What Kind of Society Shall We Have?" Richard W. Lyman, former president of the Rockefeller Foundation and now president emeritus and J. E. Wallace Sterling Emeritus Professor in the Humanities at Stanford University, reminds us of Burke's description of "the little platoons" of France that became our own way for achieving dispersion of power and the organization of mutual effort.

As we experienced the benefits of so much citizen participation, including the personal satisfactions that such service provides, we became all the more committed to this kind of participatory society. Along the way, we constantly renewed our faith in the basic intelligence and ability of people.

We have never found a better substitute for safeguarding freedom than placing responsibility in the hands of the people and expecting them to fulfill it. We can be disappointed at times in their performance, but the ultimate answer is still the democratic compact, recently beautifully and bluntly restated by John Gardner, one of the founders of INDEPENDENT SECTOR:

"Freedom and responsibility,
Liberty and duty—
That's the deal."

We can be discouraged by the complexity of today's issues and concerned that the people won't make the right decisions for themselves, but there is wisdom and comfort in Thomas Jefferson's advice: "I know of no safe depository of the ultimate powers of society, but the people themselves; and if we think them not enlightened enough to exercise their control with a wholesome discretion, the remedy is not to take it from them, but to inform their discretion by education."

We really meant and continue to mean what is written in the Declaration of Independence. We do believe in the rights and power of the people, and these convictions cause us to stand up and be counted on a broad array of issues and to cherish and fiercely defend the freedoms of religion, speech, and assembly.

If we accept that our patterns and levels of participation and generosity contribute importantly to our national life, it then becomes essential to understand and nurture the roots that give rise to such pluralism. One of our basic jobs is to be sure that the American people understand that there is this third way by which we address our national problems and aspirations. A student can go through a good education and never really grasp what this third sector means to us as a people.

In my own regular meetings with groups, I find an alarming lack of awareness of the importance of the sector in giving people an opportunity to be unique as individuals and as a society. Young people in particular are often cynical about giving and volunteering as well as about philanthropic and voluntary organizations. Yet these are the same people who appropriately remind us how important it is to "do your own thing" or "control your own destiny" or "be empowered." It is often through our voluntary organizations that these opportunities take hold.

. . . .

Most of the great citizen movements of our society have had their origins in the independent sector, for example, the abolition of slavery, civil rights, public schooling, public libraries, and opportunities for the handicapped. Some who led those efforts were viewed as unpopular, troublesome, rabble-rousing, and maybe even dangerous. One of our largest responsibilities is to protect the freedoms that will allow their successors to establish the new causes of tomorrow. There is no greater danger to our liberty than allowing those in power to have any great control over their potential reformers.

Speaking to the issue of independence, John Gardner has said:

> Perhaps the most striking feature of the sector is its relative freedom from constraints and its resulting pluralism. Within the bounds of the law, all kinds of people can pursue any idea or program they wish. Unlike government, an independent sector group need not ascertain that its idea or philosophy is supported by some large constituency, and unlike the business sector, they do not need to pursue only those ideas which will be profitable. If a handful of people want to back a new idea, they need seek no larger consensus.
>
> Americans have always believed in pluralism—the idea that a free nation should be hospitable to many sources of initiative, many kinds of institutions, many conflicting beliefs, and many competing economic units. Our pluralism allows individuals and groups to pursue goals that they themselves formulate, and out of that pluralism has come virtually all of our creativity.
>
> Institutions of the nonprofit sector are in a position to serve as the guardians of intellectual and artistic freedom. Both the commercial and political marketplaces are subject to leveling forces that may threaten standards of excellence. In the nonprofit sector, the fiercest champions of excellence may have their say. So may the champions of liberty and justice.

Beyond the urgent causes and crusades, the independent sector simply provides people a chance to do their own thing—to be different—to be a bit freer—to be unique. In an INDEPENDENT SECTOR Occasional Paper entitled "The Third Sector: Keystone of a Caring Society," Waldemar Nielsen, drawing on his book *The Endangered Sector*, summarized the variety of interests that Americans freely pursue through their voluntary organizations:

> If your interest is people, you can help the elderly by a contribution to the Grey Panthers; or teenagers through the Jean Teen Scene of Chicago; or young children through your local nursery school; or everyone by giving to the Rock of All Ages in Philadelphia.
>
> If your interest is animals, there is the ASPCA and Adopt-A-Pet; if fishes, the Isaac Walton League; if birds, the Ameri-

can Homing Pigeon Institute or the Easter Bird Banding Association.

If you are a WASP, there is the English Speaking Union and the Mayflower Descendants Association; if you have a still older association with the country, there is the Redcliff [Chipewa] Fund of the Museum of the American Indian.

If your vision is local, there is the Cook County Special Bail Project and Clean Up the Ghetto in Philadelphia; if national, there is America the Beautiful; if global, there is the United Nations Association; if celestial, there are the Sidewalk Astronomers of San Francisco.

If you are interested in tradition and social continuity, there is the society for the Preservation of Historic Landmarks and the Portland Friends of Cast Iron Architecture; if social change is your passion there is Common Cause; and, if that seems too sober for you, there is the Union of Radical Political Revolutionary Satire in New York.

If your pleasure is music, there is a supermarket of choices—from Vocal Jazz to the Philharmonic Society to the American Guild of English Hand Bellringers.

If you don't know quite what you want, there is Get Your Head Together, Inc. of Glen Ridge, New Jersey. If your interests are contradictory, there is the Great Silence Broadcasting Foundation of California. If they are ambiguous, there is the Tombstone Health Service of Arizona.

Beyond the figures, activities, and causes served, this participation and pluralism have had great influence on the kind of people we are.

More than 250 years ago, Cotton Mather, in "Bonifacious—Essays To Do Good," preached that doing good was sound policy, an honor, a privilege, an incomparable pleasure, and a reward in itself." He also said that, "Pious example, moral leadership, voluntary effort, and private charity are the means by which competing and conflicting interests in society might be brought into harmony."

In the chapter entitled "Raising Money" in *Up From Slavery*, Booker T. Washington concludes, "While the work of going from door to door and from office to office is hard, disagreeable, and costly in bodily strength, it has some compensations—in giving one an opportunity to meet some of the best people in the world—to be more correct, I think I should say the best people in the world. When one takes a broad survey of the country, he will find that the most useful and influential people in it are those who take the deepest interest in institutions that exist for the purpose of making the world better."

What comes through from all of the great citizen movements of our history is that the participation, the caring, the evidence that people can make a difference add wonderfully to the spirit of our society. Inez Haynes Irwin, in her book *The Last Days of the Fight for Women's Suffrage*, repeatedly refers to the *spirit* of those women, not only in deciding on the task and accomplishing it, but in terms of what their success meant to them as human beings. "They developed a sense of devotion to their ideal of freedom which would have stopped short of no personal sacrifice, not death itself. They developed a sense of comradeship for each other which was half love, half admiration and all reverence. In summing up a fellow worker, they speak first of her spirit, and her spirit is always *beautiful*, or *noble* or *glorious*."

It is clear that when people make the effort, not only are causes and other people helped, but something very special happens to the giver, too, and in the combination the community and the nation take on a spirit of compassion, comradeship, and confidence.

In a survey of the literature related to voluntary effort, I came across a remarkable lesson from the 1844 edition of *McGuffey's Reader*. It is still one of the best descriptions of why people must care about their neighbors and others. Entitled "True and False Philanthropy," it starts with a "Mr. Fantom" talking about global designs for doing good while a "Mr. Goodman" tries to get Fantom to focus on needs closer to home. For two pages, Goodman brings up a great many immediate needs of society, but Fantom disparages the attention each would take away from his sweeping solutions to society's problems.

Mr. Goodman says: "But one must begin to love somewhere and I think it is as natural to love one's own family, and to do good in one's own neighborhood, as to anybody else. And if every man in every family, village, and country did the same, why then all the schemes would be met, and the end of one village or town where I was doing good, would be the beginning of another village where somebody else was doing good; so my schemes would jut into my neighbor's; his projects would unite with those of some other local reformer; and all would fit with a sort of dovetail exactness."

Mr. Fantom snorts: "Sir, a man of large views will be on the watch for great occasions to prove his benevolence."

And Mr. Goodman concludes: "Yes, sir; but if they are so distant that he cannot reach them, or so vast that he cannot grasp them, he may let a thousand little, snug, kind, good actions slip through his fingers in the meanwhile; and so, between the great things that he cannot do, and little ones that he will not do, life passes, and nothing will be done."

Perhaps with the renewed interest there seems to be in *McGuffey's Reader*, there is a chance that "True and False Philanthropy" will get back into the schools and help trigger a fuller awareness and discussion of America's voluntary spirit.

Although it is important not to exaggerate the worth of voluntary effort and the giving that supports it, it is also important not to underestimate how much this participation means to our opportunities to be unique and free as individuals and as a society. Through our voluntary initiative and independent institutions, ever more Americans worship freely, study quietly, are cared for compassionately, experiment creatively, serve effectively, advocate aggressively, and contribute generously. These national traits are constantly beautiful and, hopefully, will remain beautifully constant.

Religion Is Central to the Nonprofit Sector

EACH TIME A NEW REPORT is issued that illustrates the generous giving of Americans, including those of low and moderate income, many if not most people downplay the significance because, as they point out, close to half of the money goes to religious institutions and somehow that isn't supposed to count.

That point of view is reinforced by the otherwise welcome new wave of researchers studying the independent sector who leave out religious congregations when measuring the sector's size and impact, as though such organizations don't really belong in examinations of what this sector does.

I argue that any comprehensive look at the sector has to include these organizations.

Three recent reports make clear that a very large part of the nonprofit sector's service to society is performed by religious congregations and that religious conviction is a primary

---

Op-Ed piece in *NonProfit Times*, June 1989.

motivator for much of the public's giving and volunteering. The numbers themselves should make it hard to ignore the significance of generosity to and through congregations.

Various studies indicate that just about half of all the funds contributed by individuals each year to all causes goes to churches, synagogues, mosques, and other religious organizations. INDEPENDENT SECTOR's recent report, "Giving and Volunteering in the United States," based on a 1988 Gallup survey of contributions in 1987, put religion's share at 52.5 percent.

That's important of itself and not surprising. However, what was less well known and understood, and is now brought out in INDEPENDENT SECTOR's second recent study, "From Belief to Commitment," which documents the community services of religious congregations, is that approximately half (46 percent) of all funds contributed to religion is used in ways that express religious conviction about service to others.

Even the other half (54 percent), which was spent on more direct practices such as worship and religious education, should not be put aside or dismissed in any analysis of the worth of voluntary initiative. After all, freedom of religious expression played a large role in the birth and growth of the nation. In addition, every religion in one form or another teaches a gospel of service and charity.

In addition to the funds that are contributed directly to congregations, another 15 percent or so is contributed to religiously affiliated colleges, homes for the aged, day-care centers, and other such service institutions, meaning that of the funds contributed by individuals, between 65 and 70 percent goes to congregations and other religious institutions. That statistic is particularly impressive when one considers that individuals account for 90 percent of all giving.

On the volunteering side, religious congregations are again the largest category. Various reports put the figure between 15 percent and 20 percent of all volunteers. "Giving and Volunteering in the United States" puts it at 15.9 percent.

Our study, "From Belief to Commitment," makes clear how very large the community services are of religious groups, dwarfing all funds contributed to and by other voluntary organizations for local human services. The report documents that religious congregations are the primary voluntary service providers for neighborhoods. It is my experience that the poorer the community, the larger that role and impact.

As the figures and their relevance to service become understood, it will no longer be possible or acceptable to leave out churches from our discussion of voluntary organizations. Henceforth, researchers, funders, and volunteers intent on identifying who makes the greatest difference will have to acknowledge the pervasive network of America's religious bodies.

Beyond the benefits to society of freedom of religious expression and the direct community services of religious congregations is the part religious conviction plays in motivating people toward service as well as its role in getting people to focus on fundamental values and the moral issues of their time.

INDEPENDENT SECTOR studies referred to earlier (and another one on press that deals specifically with underlying motivations for altruistic behavior) make clearer than has ever been documented that religious teaching and practice are the primary factors contributing to generous behavior.

Thus, it is not just that we support our congregations and their community services with time and money, but that what we have been taught about serving "the least of these my brethren" carries over to support of other voluntary institutions.

In 1980, Research and Forecast, Inc., conducted a study for the Connecticut Mutual Life Insurance Company on "American Values in the '80s" which reaffirmed that religious training and orientation influence charitable behavior generally. The final report, appropriately entitled "The Impact of Belief," indicated that the 45 million Americans who are "intensely religious" (as measured by regular church going) "are far more likely to be volunteers active in the community, and contribute far more than average to charity."

Religious institutions also have been and continue to be the places where the moral issues are raised and pursued. Tocqueville saw this country's network of voluntary organizations not so much as service providers but as "the moral associations" where such values as charity and responsibility to others are taught and where the nation's crusades take root.

We don't have to ransack history for examples. Who has been more in the forefront of the public business of the homeless and the resettlement of refugees? And who has provided a forum for messengers as different as Jesse Jackson and Jerry Falwell—messengers so different that people want to narrow the definition of religion to protect us from the other side?

The more I study American patterns and levels of civic participation, the more I become aware how much of the country's traditions of community service and advocacy relate to the earliest activities of churches and to the initial and continuing protection of the freedoms of religion, assembly, and speech.

Despite how obvious this is, people tend to set aside this whole half of the voluntary sector as though it didn't really belong, relating largely to salvation.

If we will just look at what the conscience, the meeting ground, and the organized neighborliness represented by religious congregations mean to the kind of society we are, we will understand and respect that religion is central to our nonprofit sector and to the American experience.

3

Impact of Nonprofits on Civil Society

JOHN DEWEY IN "ETHICS OF Democracy" concluded that "democracy is not an alternative to other principles of associated life. It is the idea of community life itself." Dewey's biographer, Robert Westbrook, notes that "Dewey was the most important advocate of participatory democracy, that is, of the belief that democracy as an ethical ideal calls upon men and women to build communities in which the necessary opportunities and resources are available for every individual to realize fully his or her particular capacities and powers through participation in political, social and cultural life."[1]

In "American Philanthropy and the National Character," historian Merle Curti states, "Emphasis on voluntary initiative . . . has helped give America her national character. . . . All these

---

Excerpts from a paper of the same title prepared for the Aspen Institute's Nonprofit Sector Research Fund conference on "The Nonprofit Sector and Democracy," December 1993.

philanthropic initiatives give support to the theses that philanthropy has helped to shape the national character . . . [by] implementing the idea that America is a process rather than a finished product."[2]

In *The Good Society*, Robert Bellah et al explain their title and thesis thusly: "It is central to our very notion of a good society that it is an open quest, actively involving all its members. . . . Indeed, the great classic criteria of a good society—peace, prosperity, freedom, justice—all depend today on a new experiment in democracy, a newly extended and enhanced set of democratic institutions, within which we citizens can better discern what we really want and what we ought to want to sustain a good life on this planet for ourselves and the generations to come."[3]

Robert Wuthnow's research, as summarized in *Acts of Compassion: Caring for Others and Helping Ourselves*, makes the case that "[Compassion] locates us as members of the diffuse networks of which our society is woven." At another point, the author writes: "Compassion stands for something larger than life itself. It reminds us of our humanity and therefore of the deeper qualities that are essential to our common human existence."[4]

In "A Parliament of the People," Woodrow Wilson wrote: "The whole purpose of democracy is that we may hold counsel with one another so as not to depend upon the understanding of one man, but to depend upon the counsel of all. For only as men are brought into counsel, and state their own needs and interest, can the general interests of great people be compounded into a policy suitable to all. So, at this opening of a new age, in this its day of unrest and discontent, it is our part to clear the air to bring about common counsel; to set up the *parliament of the people.*"[5]

In his keynote address to INDEPENDENT SECTOR's 1987 Research Forum on "The Constitution and the Independent Sector," David Mathews argued that "the role of the sector in bringing together people, formally and informally, to deal with shared issues makes it the most 'public' of the sectors in the context of 'public life as our shared life in all its forms.'" He then suggested that we grossly underestimate what the less formal networks of our communities mean to our interdependence, including influence on government.

Mathews provided this framework for the contributions of the sector:

1. To provide the infrastructure of our political environment...
2. To foster political socialization and develop public leadership...
3. To provide the quality of public talk, to increase our problem-solving capacity, and to generate political will...
4. To supply public power...
5. To create the public itself...

He concluded: "We think how dependent the public is on government—how much we need good government. But what we may lose sight of is how much good government needs a good public...."[6]

Robert D. Putnam in "What Makes Democracy Work?," published by the *National Civic Review* and drawn from his book *Making Democracy Work: Civic Traditions in Modern Italy*, writes: "[S]ome regions of Italy have a rich network of community associations. Their citizens are engaged by public issues and take an active role in politics. They trust one another to act fairly and obey the law. Social and political networks here are organized horizontally, not hierarchically. At the other pole are the 'uncivic' regions, where the very concept of citizenship is stunted. Engagement in social and cultural associations is meager, and the social structure is hierarchical. Public affairs is someone else's business, not mine. Laws are made to be broken, and people live in fear. Trapped by these vicious circles, nearly everyone feels exploited and unhappy—and democracy fails."[7]

. . . .

When Vaclav Havel received the Onassis Prize for Man and Mankind, he concluded his acceptance speech with these words: "The modern era is at its height, and if we are not to perish of our modernness we have to rehabilitate the human dimension of citizenship...."[8]

When I became president of the National Council on Philanthropy, and later after INDEPENDENT SECTOR was formed, I found I was called on regularly to provide briefings, testimony, articles, and speeches about the role and impact of philanthropic and voluntary initiative. However, I found that there were relatively few wonderful written examples that brought the generalizations to life. That's when Ann O'Connell and I set out to pull together specific tales of gifts and volunteers that seemed to us to have made a very large difference in many different fields.

For *Philanthropy in Action*, we amassed about 2,500 examples of gifts that struck us as being both good examples and good tales that helped bring philanthropy alive. From these, we chose approximately 300 within thirteen disparate categories, including: 1) To Discover New Frontiers of Knowledge; 2) To Support and Encourage Excellence; 3) To Enable People to Exercise Their Potential; 4) To Relieve Human Misery; 5) To Preserve and Enhance Democratic Government and Institutions; 6) To Make Communities a Better Place to Live; 7) To Nourish the Spirits; 8) To Create Tolerance, Understanding, and Peace Among People; and 9) To Remember the Dead.[9]

For *Volunteers in Action*, we collected about 4,000 examples that we thought helped tell the story of the sector and sifted these to about 400 examples in the following categories: 1) Serving Those Most in Need; 2) Lifting People Toward Self-Reliance; 3) Advocating and Empowering; 4) Cooperating in Mutual Dependence and Assistance; 5) Exercising Religious Belief; 6) Serving Many Other Causes and Places—From Arts to Zoos; and 7) Serving Many Other Causes and Places—From Kindergartens to Cemeteries.[10]

In the introduction to *Volunteers in Action*, we wrote: "[I]t is the work of millions of volunteers that adds up to the compassion, spirit, and power that are the quintessential characteristics of voluntary action in America. Everyone can make a difference, and many, many people do.

"Most of our examples are contemporary, or at least recent. In some cases we have gone back in time to provide chronology or to make a point, but generally we have sought to help the reader relate to these people. We also wanted to illustrate the point that volunteering is alive and well.

"As with *Philanthropy in Action*, we don't pretend that this book is a definitive record of the subject. Both books are attempts to pull together random examples that might be fun to know about and that might help tell the story of what philanthropy and voluntary action do. This book does not represent a scientific sampling, nor have we attempted to verify that all the people have done what someone said they did. That kind of test will have to await more scholarly studies. For now, these examples, however random and anecdotal, represent a very strong indication that philanthropy and voluntary action have made and continue to make a large difference in almost every area of human endeavor."

Notes

1. Robert B. Westbrook, *John Dewey and American Democracy*. Ithaca, New York: Cornell University Press, 1991.

2. Merle E. Curti, "American Philanthropy and the National Character," *American Quarterly 10*, No. 4 (Winter 1958): 420-437.

3. Robert N. Bellah, Richard Madsen, William M. Sullivan, Ann Swidler, and Steven M. Tipton, *The Good Society*. New York: Alfred A. Knopf, 1991.

4. Robert Wuthnow, *Acts of Compassion: Caring for Others and Helping Ourselves*. Princeton, New Jersey: Princeton University Press, 1991.

5. Woodrow Wilson, "A Parliament of the People," 1912 campaign address, reprinted by *Kettering Review* (Fall 1988), Dayton, Ohio.

6. David Mathews, "The Independent Sector and the Political Responsibilities of the Public," Spring Research Forum, INDEPENDENT SECTOR, Washington, D.C., 1988.

7. Robert D. Putnam, "What Makes Democracy Work?," *National Civic Review* (Spring 1993), Denver, Colorado.

8. Vaclav Havel, Acceptance Speech, Onassis Prize for Man and Mankind (Athens, May 24, 1993).

9. Brian O'Connell, *Philanthropy in Action*. New York: The Foundation Center, 1987.

10. Brian O'Connell and Ann Brown O'Connell, *Volunteers in Action*. New York: The Foundation Center, 1989.

4
Philanthropy in Action

WHEN I WAS GROWING UP in Worcester, Massachusetts, we had a neighbor who was considered odd because he kept trying to put rockets in the air. Almost nobody thought he could do it and the few who did were worried that he would cause perpetual rain or bring the sky falling in or shoot an angel.

Robert H. Goddard was known derisively as "the moon man." In 1920 he had made the laughable prediction that a rocket could go to the moon. For years the only money he had for research came from his own pocket. His first grant came in 1917, a $5,000 gift from the Hodgkins Fund of the Smithsonian Institution for "constructing and launching a high altitude rocket." Nine years later his modest attempt to fulfill the terms of that grant rose 41 feet and flew for 2.5 seconds—just far enough to encourage Goddard and short enough to discourage funders.

From *Philanthropy In Action,* by Brian O'Connell. New York: The Foundation Center, 1987.

In 1928 a larger model blasted off, literally and figuratively. The explosion did send his missile 100 feet up but started a fire several hundred feet wide. Most of the press attention focused on the fire, but a few stories marveled at the accomplishment, and one of these was read by Mrs. Harry Guggenheim.

The history of Goddard's rocketry and the Guggenheim's support is nicely captured in Milton Lomask's *Seed Money: The Guggenheim Story*. Lomask writes that Harry Guggenheim consulted no less than Charles Lindbergh on the practicality of Goddard's ideas. Lindbergh first satisfied himself and then the Guggenheims that Goddard might be on to something big, then he made the case to Harry's father, Daniel Guggenheim. Mr. Lomask gives Lindbergh's recollection of their 1930 discussion:

Mr. Dan: "Then you believe rockets have an important future?"

Lindbergh: "Probably. Of course one is never certain."

"But you think so. And this professor, he looks like a pretty capable man?"

"As far as I can find out, Mr. Guggenheim, he knows more about rockets than anybody else in the country."

"How much money does he need?"

"He'd like to have $25,000 a year for a four-year project."

"Do you think he can accomplish enough to make it worth his time?"

"Well, it's taking a chance, but if we're ever going to get beyond the limits of airplanes and propellers, we'll probably have to go to rockets. It's a chance but, yes, I think it's worth taking."

"All right, I'll give him the money."

For the next two years, Goddard worked full-time at a test site in Roswell, New Mexico. When Daniel Guggenheim died, the rest of the grant could not be paid and the Roswell project was abandoned.

Fortunately, once the estate was settled, and the Daniel and Florence Guggenheim Foundation was established, one of the first grants, renewed for nine successive years, was for $18,000 for the continuation of Goddard's work at Roswell. Lomask reports that the culmination of those years was a rocket that became "the parent of all the 9000 mile Atlases and Redstones that will ever fly, all the Sputniks that will ever circle planet earth, all the Project Mercury, Saturn and Jupiter capsules that will ever soar to Venus, Moon and Mars. . . . "

There don't seem to be figures on how much Goddard received from various sources for his lifetime of research, but it probably was a good deal less than a half million dollars. Matched against what his work has led to, it is appropriate that the Guggenheim story is told under the heading "Seed Money."

At the beginning of his book *American Philanthropy*, historian Robert H. Bremner traces American generosity all the way back to the literal seed corn.

> From other Indians, pioneer white settlers obtained a wealth of practical assistance in the difficult task of adjusting to life in an alien land. The names of most of these benefactors are forgotten, but one at least is familiar to every schoolboy. Squanto, who . . . proved a special instrument sent by God for the good of the enfeebled, bewildered Pilgrims. He taught them, in the words of William Bradford, how to set their corn, where to take fish, and to procure other commodities, and was also their pilot to bring them to unknown places for their profit, and never left them till he died.

Three hundred and fifty years later, the Ford Foundation provided funding for a pilot project that developed into the Native American Rights Fund.

Speaking of the Ford Foundation's support, the Fund's executive director, John Echohawk, says:

> . . . it cannot be stated strongly enough what a difference that backing meant to the Indian rights movement. For the first time Native Americans were guaranteed quality advocacy for a sustained period to successfully advance their rights. What a difference that knowledge makes in the legal arena—both to our opponents—as well as to Native Americans. . . . For the first time, America's Indians are being assured that the White man's system can work for, and not just against them.

Philanthropy, being so much a part of the country's pluralism, operates in thousands of different ways: many inspirational, some silly, and a few downright dangerous. Contrast the Rockefeller Foundation's "Green Revolution," which increased the food supply for millions, with the Emma S. Robinson Christmas Dinner Trust Fund for Horses or Garrett Smith's funding of John Brown's raid on Harpers Ferry, and you have some feel for the scope.

Charles Pratt was a cautious philanthropist. When he designed the buildings for Pratt Institute he did it "suchwise that in case his educational purpose failed, he might readily convert the premises into a factory."

In *Ladies Bountiful*, William G. Rogers, referring to patrons of artists, comments on assistance given to James Joyce by the "eminent and self-sacrificing angel, Lady Gregory," for whom Joyce coined this limerick:

> *There was a kind lady called Gregory*
> *Said, "Come to me, poets in beggary,"*
> *But found her imprudence*
> *When thousands of students*
> *Cried, "All, we are all in that category."*

When word reached the East Coast in 1885 that Leland Stanford was considering founding a college in the West to rank with Harvard and Columbia, a New York newspaper responded, "California needs a great university about like Switzerland needs a great navy."

The rest of the story is well known, except perhaps one often overlooked point, that from the start, Stanford University was to admit women, which brought one more response from the East: "Can you imagine such audacity as that?"

At a recent gathering of college presidents, I was fortunate to sit next to Dick Wood, the president of Earlham College. In the course of conversation, he mentioned that he had been a Danforth Fellow, and when I asked about the experience he responded emphatically that the fellowship had been the most profound influence on his professional development and one of the most important on his personal life. He said he was not alone in feeling that way; he and a very large number of Danforth and

Kent Fellows had long ago created the Society for Values and Higher Education so that they could maintain their contacts and thus sustain their mutual growth.

In his 1951 Founders' Day address, "The Power of Freedom," at Johns Hopkins University, Henry Allen Moe, early leader of the John Simon Guggenheim Memorial Foundation, spoke of the role of philanthropy in the support of talent:

> ... here and there stands out one who exemplifies, in Bertrand Russell's words, "all the noon-day brightness of human genius." ... To develop and bring to their highest possible exercise the capacities of individual persons to make that voyage is, quite obviously, the world's most needed result. Only thus shall we add that knowledge and understanding which is our best hope for survival and progress. All universities and all foundations should know they miss all their best opportunities if they fail to recognize that this should be their one goal, and it is the only goal within their reach.

If it's true that God loves a cheerful giver, he must have a particularly warm spot for Doctor D. K. Pearsons, who gave everything away, and did it in good spirit. For example, when Pearsons sent the enormous sum of $50,000 to Montpelier Seminary in Vermont in 1912, he appended this note:

> Fifty-thousand dollars, farewell! You have been in my keeping for many years, and you have been a faithful servant. . . . Go into the keeping of young men and God's blessings go with you! Do your duty, and give the poor boys and girls of Vermont a fair chance.

Another devoted Christian and clever philanthropist was Elias Boudinot, founding president of the American Bible Society, who provided a bequest to the Society for "the purchase of spectacles for poor old people, it being in vain to give a Bible to those who cannot obtain the means of reading it."

. . . .

Philanthropy is often at its best when it fulfills the role of enhancing democratic government and other democratic institutions. For example, less than 100 years ago, a few hardy individuals and institutions established what became the professional field of public administration.

The Citizens' Union was created in 1897 and the New York Bureau of Municipal Research followed in 1904. Their establishment stemmed from concerns about corrupt and inefficient city government. In the case of the New York Bureau, a few courageous individuals had finally decided to confront the corruption and power of Tammany Hall. Their objectives were simply stated, but almost impossible to fulfill. They wanted to create citizen interest, involvement, and control in the exercise of democratic government; to attract able people into government service; and to study how to achieve effective and responsible governance. The bosses and clubs that exercised iron-fisted control in almost all major cities were bound to resist. The story of the organizations that first fought for reform and of the thousands of civic associations and societies for good government that followed demonstrate how important it is that private philanthropy and voluntary action remain independent of government and how substantial their impact can be as a result of that independence. In *New York Bureau of Municipal Research: Pioneer in Government Administration,* Jane S. Dahlberg indicates that there were many citizens, professionals, and supporters who provided support, but the funder who remained steadfast was Mrs. E. H. Harriman.

Much later, when the Bureau sought to establish a training school for public service, Mrs. Harriman donated the necessary money. Dahlberg writes:

> Mrs. Harriman returned from a visit late in 1910, enthusiastic about the caliber of men in the British Government's Career Service. She thought that more young men from families of influence in this country should enter public life. She offered to contribute money to Harvard, Yale or Columbia for training of such men for government service, but was scornfully turned down as politics was considered dirty at worst and non-academic at best.

Mrs. Harriman instead gave the money to establish what became the New York Training School for Public Service, the prototype for schools of public service that thereafter began to spring up across the country.

One of the newer lessons about philanthropy involves the breadth of ways that corporate philanthropy is becoming involved.

About four years ago, at a Council on Foundations meeting, Alex Plinio, then director of contributions for Prudential, gave a paper with a title something like "Fourteen Ways that Companies Provide Noncash Assistance to Voluntary Organizations." I urged him to expand it into a more formal article and told him that INDEPENDENT SECTOR would be pleased to publish it as part of a series of Occasional Papers. About a year later, I asked Alex how it was coming, and he said he had run into the interesting problem that he kept finding new examples that should be included. By then, he was up to "Twenty-Nine Ways . . . " He had also been promoted to vice president for public service and president of the Prudential Foundation, so he would have even less time to work on the paper. Finding the idea more interesting than ever and sharing his frustration with the time constraints he faced, I said we would provide him with some research and editorial assistance. Another year went by, and I explained to him that we really should be getting something published. This time Alex said that between his own efforts and those of Joanne Scanlon, the part-time research assistant, he was coming across all kinds of new information that really should be included. By then, he was up to "Forty-One Ways . . . "

Six months later, out of eagerness to have this important resource document published and seeing my offer of modest help reach a not-so-modest level, I said we absolutely had to go with what we had. The result was Plinio and Scanlon's excellent *Resource Raising: The Role of Non-Cash Assistance in Corporate Philanthropy*, which contains, in six categories, forty-nine types of assistance and more than one hundred examples. At that, Alex Plinio still says, "You know, Brian, I wish we hadn't rushed that into print, because it's still very incomplete."

Their paper graphically illustrates how different corporate philanthropy is from the work of private foundations. *Resource Raising* contains information about an extraordinary variety of in-kind gifts or subsidies that corporations are currently providing to nonprofit organizations. These include gifts of land; computer tie-ins; piggy-back advertising; dispute resolution and negotiation services; energy conservation audits; product and marketing consultation; survey development and analysis; gifts of trees, horses, and seeds; no-interest or low-interest loans; meeting and conference facilities; and staff and volunteer training.

As important as in-kind gifts are, they are still only a supplement to the generous dollar support the corporations represent. I was reminded of this during one of the public meetings of the Minnesota Council on Foundations when one of the corporate speakers went on and on about how much was being done by a growing number of companies to provide noncash support. The already lively discussion ended with applause and whistles when one of the voluntary agency representatives rose to observe: "With all due respect for your noncash help, I hope you won't get so carried away with it that you forget the cash!"

Perhaps the most universally applauded grants to America's communities were Andrew Carnegie's gifts of libraries. He gave more than $40 million to fund 1,680 of them. Despite how obvious it is to us now that those grants proved vital to learning, they were often viewed with suspicion and hostility. Throughout the country, community leaders denounced these facilities as Carnegie's way of forcing towns to do what he wanted them to do. They said that they saw through his condition that if he paid for the building, they would have to pay for the books and maintain the service. In place after place, the gifts were attacked on the pretext that ordinary people didn't need to read, or would steal the books, or should be satisfied with their school texts. In his book *Philanthropy's Role in Civilization,* Arnaud C. Marts reports that in one community these signs appeared:

RATEPAYERS!
RESIST THIS FREE LIBRARY DODGE
AND SAVE YOURSELVES FROM THE BURDEN OF $6,000
OF ADDITIONAL TAXATION!

Marts reports that for many years even the progressive state of Massachusetts prohibited municipalities from taxing people for libraries.

The history of philanthropy is full of grants that we can't imagine were controversial, but which in their time seemed radical and ill advised. Massachusetts was on the better side of the controversy involving kindergartens, but most other states saw the movement as sinister. Elizabeth Peabody of Boston, a sister of Horace Mann, donated her own funds and raised money from her friends to establish the first English-language kindergarten. Arnaud Marts writes: "In 1859, another specialized field of education . . . the kindergarten was opened up by private initiative. It was first organized as a charity kindergarten for poor and uncared for waifs but was soon discovered to be an excellent form of preschool training for normal children."

It is hard to fathom that kindergartens could have been threatening to anybody, but Mrs. Peabody started a long and bitter dispute. Her attackers said that children that age were too young to learn and belonged in the home anyway; that her idea undermined the family, transferred to the state a private responsibility, and would raise taxes that were already too high or were needed for *real* public services. The cries of bloated government and encouraging family dependence on government caused many states to enact laws prohibiting the use of school funds or other taxes to be used on children of kindergarten age. It took almost fifty years for what we now consider such an obviously beneficial program to gain acceptance.

A hundred years after Mrs. Peabody's first kindergarten, Mr. Carnegie's foundation, the Carnegie Corporation of New York, and others took the idea a step further by funding Head Start, a program for disadvantaged children of pre-kindergarten age, and thirty years later the fur is still flying. I suppose day care will be next.

Sometimes the hardest tasks look easier than they are and turn out to require several lifetimes of investment. Early in this century, Carnegie established the Endowment for International Peace and provided his trustees with advice on what to do with his money when they had finished the job. The endowment was to have been the capstone of Carnegie's philanthropic endeavors, but even his optimism and resources were no match for serious international problems. Philip E. Mosely, writing on "International Affairs" in Warren Weaver's *U.S. Philanthropic Foundations,* captures nicely the Carnegie spirit:

> In establishing the Carnegie Endowment for International Peace in 1910, Andrew Carnegie sincerely believed that the permanent elimination of wars and prospect of wars might well be achieved in the lifetime of men then living. He directed the Trustees, when that happy state had been achieved, to apply the Endowment's resources to solve other major problems of mankind.

What followed, of course, was not peace but two slaughtering world wars; the development of nuclear weapons; Korea, Vietnam, the Middle East, and a world that could explode at any moment. Andrew Carnegie, where are you?

It is encouraging that, seventy-five years later, Mr. Carnegie's foundation, the Carnegie Corporation of New York, is picking up the challenge with a new endeavor to try to end war.

. . . .

It is unreasonable and even inappropriate to expect that all philanthropic organizations will be on the "cutting edge." While much of the good that philanthropy does is accomplished at the edge, many funders find themselves encouraging organizations toward excellence, intervening where human misery is greatest, or nourishing the human spirit.

Philanthropy plays many different roles in our society, but its central value is the extra dimension it provides for seeing and doing things differently. Philanthropy doesn't take the place of government or other basic institutions, but its impact is clear in just about every field of endeavor, including fields as different as architecture, health, human rights, historic preservation, ballet, neighborhood empowerment, agriculture, rocketry, physics, the homeless, astronomy—and peace.

Oliver Wendell Holmes observed, "Philanthropists are commonly grave, occasionally grim and not very rarely morose." From my long review of their accomplishments, I think philanthropists have a lot of reasons to be happier with what they do.

In Perpetuity or Just for a While?

In his "Principles of Public Giving," Julius Rosenwald acknowledged that Alexander Hamilton was a wise man, but added:

> Yet it was Hamilton who drafted the will of Robert Richard Randall, who in the first years of the last century left a farm to be used as a haven for superannuated sailors. A good many years ago the courts were called upon to construe the word "sailor" to include men employed on steamships. Even so, the Fund for Snug Harbor, I am assured, vastly exceeds any reasonable requirement for the care of retired seafarers. The farm happened to be situated on Fifth Avenue, New York. Today it is valued at $30 or $40 million.

From Chapter 9, "To Remember the Dead," *Philanthropy in Action*, by Brian O'Connell. New York: The Foundation Center, 1987.

Rosenwald's "Principles" were first published in *The Atlantic Monthly* in May 1929, and drew considerable response, with particular focus on Rosenwald's opposition "to gifts in perpetuity for any purpose."

Rosenwald offered these additional examples to make his point:

> I have heard of a fund which provides a baked potato at each meal for each young woman at Bryn Mawr, and of another, dating from one of the great famines, which pays for half a loaf of bread deposited each day at the door of each student in one of the colleges at Oxford. Gifts to educational institutions often contain provisions which are made absurd by the advance of learning. An American university has endowed lectureship on coal gas as the cause of malarial fever. ... The list of these precisely focused gifts which have lost their usefulness could be extended into volumes, but I am willing to rest the case on Franklin and Hamilton. With all their sagacity, they could not foresee what the future would bring. The world does not stand still. Anyone old enough to vote has seen revolutionary changes in the mechanics of living, and these changes have been accomplished and abetted by changing points of view toward the needs and desires of our fellow men.
>
> I do not know how many millions of dollars have been given in perpetuity for the support of orphan asylums. The Hershey endowment alone is said to total $40,000,000 and more. Orphan asylums began to disappear about the time the old-fashioned wall telephone went out.

True to his convictions, Rosenwald directed that his own fund should be entirely spent "within 25 years of the time of my death." The trustees obviously caught Rosenwald's spirit, for the fund was fully expended in fourteen years and closed in 1946.

Rosenwald's daughter, Edith R. Stern, and her children carried on the example of time-limited trusts. A May 19, 1986, *New York Times* story told of the closing of their fund:

> After a half-century of philanthropy, the Stern Fund of New York has spent itself out of existence and has thrown a party to celebrate.

> The ending had been planned from the beginning, in 1936 in New Orleans. The founders, Edith and Edgar Stern, did not want their fund to spend money perpetuating itself.
> ... The ending was in keeping with a family tradition. Mrs. Stern, who died in 1980, was a daughter of Julius Rosenwald, a founding partner of Sears, Roebuck & Company.

The Rosenwald and Stern Funds represent one alternative to perpetual trusts, but there are many other variations and models. For instance, Mr. Rosenwald, along with Calvin Coolidge and Alfred E. Smith, was a trustee of the Hubert Fund, which decided on immediate distribution of its assets.

Frederick P. Keppel, in *The Foundation: Its Place in American Life*, reports that:

> The trustees appointed by the late Payne Whitney, instead of creating a foundation, as they might have done under the terms of Mr. Whitney's will, announced the immediate distribution of the principal sum entrusted to them, amounting to nearly $20–$36 million, among certain institutions in which Mr. Whitney had already shown an interest and had supported with characteristic generosity.

Edward A. Filene gave his trustees the option to spend part or all of the principal.

Several years ago, the Rockefeller brothers decided to direct approximately half of the assets of the Rockefeller Brothers Fund to the favorite institutions of each brother and their sister.

The Fleischmann Foundation grew to more than $100 million before the trustees began to fulfill the request of the donor, Max. C. Fleischmann, who asked that the fund be expended within twenty years after the death of his wife.

A compromise between a perpetual fund, with the disadvantages Rosenwald foresaw, and indefinite investment, is the gift to a community trust. Frederick Goff, founder of the community foundation movement, was motivated in part by his dislike for self-perpetuating philanthropy. His solution was to encourage leaving money in perpetuity, but to a board that was not self-perpetuating and indeed was designed to reflect contemporary community priorities. As Goff put it: "The community foundation is the best way to defeat the 'dead hand.'"

When I compare all the good arguments against perpetual trusts (the foundation's purpose gets out of date; the staff becomes so professional that the original purposes are suffocated; control of the foundation by "the dead hand"; and so on) with the relatively few foundation dollars there are—certainly compared to government expenditures—I tend to come down on the side of perpetuity. I have repeatedly come across the enormous current impact of such foundations as Ford, Carnegie, Rockefeller, Commonwealth, and Kellogg. Had they all gone the way of Rosenwald, Fleischmann, Hubert, and Whitney, I wonder if there would be nearly the positive influence of this "extra dimension" on society today.

I find myself wishing very much that the General Education Board were around today to deal with the issues of racism and unequal opportunity. When I look at the growth of the John Simon Guggenheim Memorial Foundation, which still has more than $100 million in assets (after spending even more than that in interest), and which still has great influence on scholarship and international understanding, I wonder if the case really holds up that we would have been better off if that money had all been spent by 1950.

Pluralism is one of philanthropy's most attractive assets. Certain donors may want their estates to be dispersed immediately; others may wish to establish time-limited trusts; while still others may prefer gifts in perpetuity. All of these should be options for giving money to strengthen the future fabric of society.

From Service to Advocacy to Empowerment

THE DEVELOPMENT OF VOLUNTEERING in America has now evolved through four principal transition and growth stages. During each, the degree and nature of the volunteer effort have changed significantly.

The first stage took place during the period of colonization in the early days of this country, when banding together was necessary for survival, with the church and the town council having dominant roles in promoting people's humanity to people.

The Civil War marked the beginning of the second stage, which extended for almost three-quarters of a century into the 1930s. These years saw a significant transition from individual charity to organized voluntaryism. Many of the organizations generally identified with volunteering were established in this

---

Excerpts from an article of the same title in "Social Casework" (1978) and adapted from "Voluntarism: Today and Tomorrow," a speech presented at the biennial convention of the Family Service Association of America in 1977.

period, including the Red Cross, the Young Men's Christian Association (YMCA), the National Conference on Social Welfare (NCSW), Chicago's Hull House, the American Public Health Association, the Mental Health Association, the Family Service Association of America, and many, many more. For the most part, these organizations represented only tentative beginnings, with their relatively small groups trying to spark widespread citizen interest in significant problems.

During the First World War, this second stage of organized citizen effort burgeoned and there emerged an increased need for properly organizing this help. As during the Civil War, this voluntary spirit was largely sustained into the postwar years for relief programs and for an increasing list of domestic issues. The American Hearing Society was formed in 1919, the Crippled Children and Adults Society in 1921, the American Foundation for the Blind in 1921, and Planned Parenthood in 1922, followed by a whole new wave of veterans' organizations. The Depression years saw thousands of local relief activities established. During the 1930s, the Community Chest movement developed. It was during this period, also, that the balance of roles between government and voluntary activity began to be actively studied and the multiplicity of private organizations began to be of concern. Almost overnight, charity and service had become big business, and volunteering hit a numerical all-time high.

With the establishment of the March of Dimes in 1938, the third major transition and growth stage for organized citizen participation occurred. Volunteer service, which had largely been the province of the upper classes, suddenly was open to middle America. Philanthropy, which also had been the province of the wealthy, gave way to the nickel-and-dime collections and payroll deductions that today are the cornerstones of American giving. World War II and the postwar period into the fifties lent great impetus to this third stage of citizen participation by the very number of new agencies that were developed and the breadth of the causes they represented. This was a period of staggering growth in the numbers of nonprofit organizations and of the people who rallied to them. In the 1950s, voluntary health and welfare organizations represented the greatest source of volunteering the world had ever known. For the most part, they were made up of new middle-class recruits who started with doorbell ringing or other fund-raising roles and quickly moved into leadership positions.

This period of volunteering is increasingly known as the time of the "Gentle Legions," after the book of that title by Richard Carter in which he describes the impact of the March of Dimes and the new wave of voluntary health agencies on American philanthropy and volunteering.[1]

Within just twenty-five years, however, there has been a transition to a fourth stage, which includes the largest step forward in citizen involvement. In the 1960s, participatory democracy suddenly began to include all parts of society. Americans are now organizing to influence every conceivable aspect of our human condition. They are increasingly willing to stand up and be counted on almost any public issue. They organize to fight zoning changes, approve bond issues, oppose or support abortion, improve garbage collection, expose overpricing, approve water fluoridation, enforce equal rights, and protest wars. And, in the process, Americans raise money and vote for a staggering array of causes. Today, a far greater proportion of the population is involved in volunteer efforts than at any time in our history. In a study entitled "Americans Volunteer," the United States Department of Labor demonstrates how Americans are involved in volunteer service:

> A new consciousness of domestic deprivation, the beginning of racial militancy and a rising affluence that permits increasing leisure have recently induced considerable growth and change in the traditional picture of the volunteer. Witness the legions of youth and young adults who spend several hours every week in helping youngsters learn to read. One remarkable aspect of the change is that many customary recipients of the volunteers' service are now serving their own and their community's interests: The young, the old, the handicapped, and the poor are serving as volunteers themselves. There are: (1) more volunteers, (2) different kinds of volunteers, (3) different kinds of functions, and (4) different channels for the delivery of their services.[2]

Columnist James Reston terms the change "the quiet revolution." He points out that:

> What is happening now is that the model for action established during the civil rights battles of the 1960s is beginning to be applied to other fields.... Citizen groups are forming to protect the environment, improve their communities, to challenge the assumptions and priorities of their elected officials, to defend the average consumer from the commercial gougers, and to work in many other ways for the improvement of American life.[3]

One of the most encouraging developments is that volunteering now includes every economic group. Participatory democracy—which had been the exclusive role first of the upper classes and then later of the upper and middle classes—has finally broadened to include all parts of society.

Why, then, in the face of all the evidence of caring and service, do we increasingly hear the lament that people's humanity to people is declining as a characteristic of the American way of life? Indeed, it seems to be a dominant impression that volunteering is sharply decreasing. The answer probably lies in a strong difference of opinion about who and what activities are to be considered within the definition of volunteering. The Department of Labor report refers to *different* volunteers, *different functions, and different* channels for delivering services.[4] It is these *differences* which begin to explain the striking contrast between the view that volunteering is in a serious slump and the facts as stated in the comprehensive federal study. Although there is clearly a wave of activism in this country, the citizens involved and their causes and methods are so different from what has been traditional in the field that people viewing it from a slightly older viewpoint do not see what is happening as *volunteering*. They still view volunteering in a conventional frame of reference, while the report reflects a new frame of reference altogether. This has so bewildered the old-time volunteers and staff and so totally upset perceptions—even of who the volunteers are—that many national and community leaders still have not or cannot acknowledge the revolution. They are concerned that the power structure as they knew it is no longer intact, and they believe that if it could somehow be recreated and the city fathers restimulated to recognize their responsibility to care for community needs, things would somehow get back in balance.

Promoting an effective voluntaryism

Clearly, those who believe that volunteering is declining do not accept as volunteers the people who are immediately interested in their own problems. For example, in a meeting with an advisory council to President Nixon's Committee on Voluntary Action, I was shaken to hear the members expressing an extremely pessimistic view of the state of volunteering. After telling the group that I thought things were far better than they believed and using as examples the healthy degree of caring represented by students, blacks, welfare recipients, antiwar demonstrators, women, homosexuals, former mental patients, and others, the council members remonstrated that it was not appropriate to include as volunteers the people who have an immediate stake in the outcome of their own volunteering. Traditionally and practically, however, it is appropriate that a person serving her needs or protecting his own rights belongs—past, as with the colonial Minuteman, present, and future—in the family of volunteers.

It is a mistake to refer to our heritage of volunteering as if to suggest that altruism were the only characteristic of the history of volunteer effort. On the contrary, the traditions of volunteering evolved from a combination of the religious spirit of people's humanity to people and a heavy dose of mutual dependence and assistance. The Minutemen and the frontier families practiced basic forms of enlightened self-interest in their forms of volunteering. To portray the American history of volunteering as though it were related solely to goodness would be to ignore the widespread tradition of organized neighborliness which hardship dictated and goodness tempered.

Many of today's voluntary agencies and their leaders are struggling to return to the good old days. With the power structure exploding to every corner of the community and society, it is a tormenting business to try to pull together a consensus so that some positive movement is achieved. It is understandable that many would yearn for more orderly days. Unfortunately, this regression would represent a regrouping along outdated lines, rather than a full use of the truly exciting multiplication of people and groups who care and who are prepared to do something about their caring. Many people do not agree with the issues and tactics of today's activists and almost everyone deplores illegal practices that infringe on the rights of others, yet all who are interested in citizen participation must cheer the fact that so many people today are concerned enough to express their caring, and that our freedoms are continuing to provide these opportunities.

Happily, we have moved by stages from the days of Lord and Lady Bountiful, through the period of the elite "400" and a concentrated power structure, and are now beginning to recognize that participatory democracy is everybody's business. We owe a tremendous debt to Dorothea Dix and her kind, and to the community fathers who served so many causes, but the greatest accolades should be reserved for the here-and-now, when democracy has truly come alive with the entire population joining in the traditions of service and reform.

Effective advocacy and empowerment

The most important new direction in voluntaryism is toward spreading more power to more people. The concept of "power to the people" says it best.

Within the frame of reference of "power to the people," it is appropriate to discuss advocacy, for it is through effective advocacy that power is secured and used. It is also natural that the most important aspect of effective advocacy is now being described as empowerment.

Most of the voluntary sector has been involved in *providing* services to people in need. Many are now talking about using some, or perhaps even much, of their power, experience, and energy to try to interpret the needs of clients so that services are developed and improved by the authorities responsible for them. Both of these efforts are highly commendable. Even more important to society, however, is the movement toward empowerment—to use and transfer power so that the groups in need of service secure enough political and economic power to be able to represent themselves effectively. This is when "power to the people" takes on its greatest significance.

The following brief illustration may help to define and explain the three levels within voluntaryism: providing services, representing clients, and empowering.

Several years ago, I served as a member of the board of a large city's family service agency at a time when the community's public welfare system was coming apart. Despite the surrounding chaos, the agency's board meetings were still totally devoted to examination of the direct services of that one agency. Finally, some of the board members were able to persuade the staff and other board members that their joint knowledge of human needs, community organization, and the welfare system had to be used to bring about a humane and sensible public assistance program. The board acted in such a manner and was amazed at how quickly we were able to exert an influence. We were moving from a preoccupation with *service* to use of knowledge to *represent* those in the constituency who were public assistance clients.

Even then, however, as community organizers we were still a giant step from more effectively involving public assistance clients in their own destinies—a basic community organization principle that community organizers have to relearn constantly. Thus, the next step was to form parents' and neighborhood groups and to use these consumers increasingly as the spokespeople for the family service agency's point of view about public assistance. We were beginning to move toward empowerment.

Impediments to advocacy and empowerment

Clearly, there are multiple roles which the voluntary sector plays, but anything that compromises or detracts from efforts to influence public policy diminishes the sector's capacity to function in the role society most depends on it to perform.

As Paul H. Sherry states:

> Their [the voluntary agencies in general] role is not primarily to serve as an alternate to government, but, instead, to help keep government honest and responsible. The

primary role of voluntary associations in American life is to continually shape and reshape the vision of a more just social order, to propose programs which might lead to the manifestation of that vision, to argue for them with other contenders in the public arena, and to press for adoption and implementation. For voluntary associations to do less than that is to abdicate their civic responsibility.[5]

Even in the face of a strong personal conviction that social action is the primary role of voluntary agencies, stronger forces are pulling the voluntary sector in the direction of providing services. These forces include:

1. a preference and preoccupation with the direct service role;
2. a combination of timidity and naïveté in exercising citizen influence on public policy;
3. increased use of government funds to underwrite services, thus tying the volunteer sector further to those services and compromising them as independent advocates for the public good.

At a time when human needs are outstripping the volunteer capacity to deal with them, the preoccupation with expanding the ability of the voluntary sector to deliver services is understandable. But, to the extent that it takes volunteers away from influencing public policy, it is not commendable.

Unfortunately, it is almost axiomatic that if an agency conducts a large service program, the board and staff will constantly devote almost all their energies, enthusiasm, and other precious resources to that program. Such programs require attention; are the most satisfying; attract money; are more specific; are what they know best how to do; and very much need doing.

The only solution for the organization that must provide services and yet recognizes a responsibility to deal substantially with public policy is to invoke an *absolute* requirement that a percentage of its time (whether this be 25, 30, 50 percent, or more) be used for social action and that administrative mechanisms be set up to be sure it happens. From sad experience, I believe that unless both the conviction and the administrative mechanisms are rigid, the emphasis will move right back to service.

Fifty percent or even 25 percent may not fit with the current tax status or mission of many voluntary organizations, but there is a lot more that the voluntary sector should be doing to change those laws and interpretations, and there is a great deal more that can be done even within those restrictive laws and interpretations. The important thing is to decide what is right and how to do it. The combination of responsibility for services and anxiety about tax status will almost certainly immobilize any tentative concern for social action.

The second impediment to an adequate contribution to social policy relates to a discomfort with the role of advocacy and social action. The voluntary agency is not sure it is strong enough to make a difference, does not quite know how to go about succeeding, and finds it hard to articulate this somewhat amorphous role to funders and even to boards. The following are some characteristics of the effective social action agency:

1. A *cause* worth getting excited about.
2. *Genuine* concern for that cause.
3. An ability to keep the cause in *focus*.
4. Acceptance of *activism* as the way to make things change, with no apologies for being activists.
5. Tenacity—it is interesting to note that, after experience in the voluntary field, John Gardner concluded: "The first requirement for effective citizen action is stamina."[6]
6. Successful advocates really *understand* how their government and service systems are organized *and* changed. Blind emotion may work a few times, but a successful, sustained effort requires know-how.
7. To make a difference in any major cause there is a need for people in real *numbers*. Politicians have learned to tune out the angry shouts to determine whether there are voters behind all that noise. It helps to have power people, and the best

combination is to have both the numbers and the power people, but if a choice has to be made, take the numbers.
8. The effective social action agency must be *independent*—free to tackle anybody *or* cooperate with anybody.

The objective and tenacious pursuit of its mission will fully test whether an organization comes close to the profile of effective advocacy outlined above. In particular, the degree of independence will be revealed. At a time when, more than ever before, the influence of voluntary organizations on public policy is needed, the independence necessary to assure that influence is being threatened and eroded.

The third force pulling the voluntary sector in the direction of service and away from attention to public policy is the increased use of government funds. There is clearly a growing push for voluntary agencies to accept government funds. The forces at work include a desperate need for more services, a determination to find better ways to serve people, a broadening concern for more aspects of the human condition, a belief in the availability of alternatives, and a concern about bigness itself as well as about the relative size and influence of government and the independent sector, the financial problems of existing agencies, and the difficulties of raising money. As a result of such pressures there has already been a marked change in the availability and relative stability of government support. Short-term grants are still important, but longer-term contracts are even more significant. With a grant you can start a halfway house, but with a contract you can operate it. As useful as contracts have become, the fee for service is evolving as the multiplier. This kind of support will quickly outweigh the private income of many voluntary agencies. Recent legislative victories, including the important ones dealing with Title XX of the Social Security Act, and the impact of Medicare and Medicaid not only allow but encourage service participation by voluntary agencies and provide fees for that service. In a presentation to national agency executives in December 1975, John C. Young, commissioner of the Community Services Administration (HEW), described Title XX as "the prototype of the new federalism." He added "that Title XX isn't the wave of the future, it's the wave of the present."[7] Additional examples of such programs and related funding are the Comprehensive Employment and Training Act (CETA) manpower effort, the "Save the Streets Act" of the Juvenile Justice Program, the Law Enforcement Assistance Administration (LEAA), and the Health Systems Agencies related to comprehensive health planning. These programs and the funds they carry with them will allow many new and existing private organizations to develop desperately needed services. In the face of all this, it is almost inevitable that government funding of the voluntary sector will increase.

Although the debate on the use of government funds is still raging, the reality is that this new pattern is already established and many voluntary agencies are quickly following it. Even if one comes down on the side opposing such support, the forces pushing the other way are prevailing and all the voluntary agencies can do is to understand what is happening well enough to capitalize on the positives and try to compensate for the negatives.

The major plus in such an arrangement is that voluntary agencies will expand and establish services that will represent alternatives, innovation, responsiveness, and just plain relief for human misery. In these days, when needs and aspirations so outdistance the capacity of our institutions to deal with them, one cannot criticize such results.

The significant negative of putting substantial government money into voluntary agencies is the automatic compromise of the independence of those organizations. As valuable as the direct services of voluntary agencies are, they are still decidedly secondary to the role of the voluntary sector as independent advocate and critic. Many of the groups that accept substantial government funds will, of course, continue to perform in advocacy/critic roles, but when the real crunch develops their reliability for independence cannot be assured. Today's voluntary agency personnel are wonderfully principled and fiercely independent, but will their successor executives and boards be so alert to compromise? Will they really be willing to drop essential programs that address pressing human needs if that's the price for calling for the replacement of an inadequate public official? How many sensitive executives will *really* be ready to terminate able providers if there is a need to demonstrate that independent advocacy is even more important than our service function? How many boards proud of their services and unused to raising the private dollars to pay for them will opt for quarreling with the source of their support? And how credible will such a board's efforts be to influence appropriations if it can be tagged with even a particle of self-interest? Additionally, it is my experience that the large service provider which is substantially dependent on government funds tends to use up much of its social action time dealing with the legislation, appropriations, and administrative red tape that relate to the agency's own program.

These tests become particularly pointed when one realizes that the most likely source of government funds is usually the government agency responsible for the same area of human need and which, therefore, the voluntary sector should be monitoring. Some agonizingly important program priorities could be advanced if my own agency, for example, were willing to accept support for them from the government's Mental Health Institute, but accepting such support would automatically lead to the loss of a real measure of independence, both to criticize the institute and to go before Congress and the administration to advocate for it.

In these days of devastating deficits, there is the greatest temptation to consider the acceptance of government funds. It is hard enough to resist using them to expand, but almost impossible to refuse them to save a beautiful program that is really helping people. However, it is just such hard times that require intact independence, credibility, and a stomach for controversy.

What I see unfolding is the development, or at least the crystallization, of a whole new category of agencies somewhere in between governmental and independent ones, operating on contracts and fees, using volunteers, and having freedom of day-to-day activity. Such an arrangement will have tremendous usefulness and should be applauded and encouraged. Before being free to capitalize appropriately on an important changeover for some agencies and before clearly understanding the void that is created, it is necessary to cross one bridge that, though it is more semantic than real, nevertheless appears to span a chasm. The voluntary sector cannot effectively deal with the situation until it acknowledges the fact that agencies which accept such an arrangement will become more *of* government than independent of it. However unique the arrangement and no matter the degree of involvement of volunteer boards, the reality is that such organizations will represent only a different way by which the government fulfills its assigned obligations. Voluntary agencies fight this and government officials deny it, but if, on an ongoing basis, government is putting up most of an agency's money, that is where the ultimate accountability rests.

We are moving toward three kinds of public organizations: governmental, quasi-governmental, and independent. Let us accept the good things which the quasi-governmental organization can do and the unique ways in which it does them. Let us also begin to consider what must be done to encourage the totally independent voices of tomorrow's reformers. There are, obviously, multiple roles which the voluntary agency can play, but anything that compromises independent advocacy in public matters diminishes its capacity to function in the arena where society is most dependent on it.

Notes

1. Richard Carter, *The Gentle Legions*. New York: Doubleday, 1961.
2. U.S. Department of Labor, "Americans Volunteer." Washington, D.C.: Government Printing Office, 1969.
3. James Reston, editorial, *The New York Times* (January 5, 1971).
4. U.S. Department of Labor, "Americans Volunteer."
5. Paul H. Sherry, "America's Third Force," *Journal of Current Social Issues* 9 (July-August 1970).
6. John Gardner, *Let Us Act: We Have Learned Some Rules for Effective Action*. Washington, D.C.: Common Cause.
7. John C. Young, "The New Federalism." Speech to the United Way of America Conference, Miami, Florida, December 19, 1976.

7

Advocating and Empowering

WHEN JORGE PRIETO received an honorary degree from the University of Notre Dame, the citation read: "His tenderness to those in need has been equalled only by the ferocity of his struggle in their behalf." Dr. Prieto was described to me by the National Council of La Raza as "the perfect candidate for your search for individuals who have helped other people to be empowered." In many ways Prieto is an ideal example of all the stages of service, advocacy, and empowerment. He began as a general practitioner in two small *ranchos* in the desert around Zacatecas, Mexico, where the people were so poor that they could not pay for his services. Later he transferred his attention from the rural poor of Mexico to the urban poor of Chicago, where he rose to become head of the Cook County Department of Family Services and finally president of Chicago's Department

---

Excerpts from Chapter 4, "Advocating and Empowering," *Volunteers In Action*, by Brian and Ann B. O'Connell. New York: The Foundation Center, 1989.

of Health. In 1987 the Latino Institute established the Jorge Prieto Humanitarian Award, of which he was the first recipient. The citation said in part:

> Dr. Prieto better than anyone we know exemplifies those values which have helped the dreams and aspirations of Latinos in this country to survive. A man of deep caring and compassion, Dr. Prieto has consecrated his life both private and professional to bringing sweet comfort to the human condition. Believing that the heart must work confluently with the intellect, Dr. Prieto has expanded the scope of his giving and understanding beyond the narrow confines of his own profession to nearly all areas of human inquiry and discovery. . . .

When Odile Stern's daughter was murdered, she became involved in a mutual-help group but later launched into advocacy efforts, including gun control. In the story "From Ashes of Tragedy, Self-Help," in *The New York Times* (June 4, 1984), Fred Ferretti describes Stern's founding of Parents of Murdered Children. "Mrs. Stern continually presses members to go beyond self-help to advocacy. . . ." And she is quoted as saying, "Now I feel Michele's death has not been in vain, but in a sense it is still too late for me, I should have been in the gun control movement early!"

The New York Times story also profiles Candy Lightner, the founder of MADD (Mothers Against Drunk Driving):

> "I remember sitting in a restaurant and somebody asked me what I did," Candy Lightner said. "I didn't know. I asked the man I was with and he told me to tell them I was an advocate, an activist." This was only a few months after her daughter was killed on May 3, 1980. By May 7, the drunken driver who had killed her daughter had been arrested and MADD was formed.

. . . .

Easily the most famous of the mutual-help groups is Alcoholics Anonymous (AA). Many of its members have also been staunch advocates on issues relating to drinking. Very typical but very special was Florette White Pomeroy of San Francisco. When she died, her obituary in *The San Francisco Examiner* highlighted her activism:

> She led the way in convicing major corporations in the West to establish programs for employees who were alcoholic—not just for humane reasons, she said, but to save the firms' investment in valued employees at all levels, from the bottom to the top.
>
> Teamsters official Jack Goldberger and other labor leaders in the Bay Area won alcoholism treatment clauses in their union contracts, setting an example for labor across the country.

The obituary also noted that Pomeroy often said: "The thing that nearly destroyed me provides me now with the channel through which, for the rest of my life, I can help others."

Bette-Ann Gwathmey and her husband lost a sixteen-year-old son to cancer. She, too, originally joined a mutual-help group but went on to greater efforts to prevent tragedy from striking others. In her case, she set out to raise the millions necessary to endow a chair in pediatric cancer at the Memorial Sloan-Kettering Cancer Center in New York.

Many people who have been touched by health crises have turned to the Herculean task of founding major national organizations to provide research, education, and service relating to that illness. Jack Hausman was such a person. Jack and Ethel Hausman had a child with cerebral palsy at a time when that condition was almost totally unknown to the general public. Their story was captured in 1986 by Recollections Inc., oral historians in White Plains, New York:

> I became interested in founding the Cerebral Palsy Association of New York because nothing was known about CP, nor was there an agency of any kind to help cerebral palsy children and to help parents cope with the tremendous challenge of caring for a cerebral palsy child. It was costing

us so much to take care of Peter, and Ethel wondered how families with little or no money could manage. In 1946, Ethel spotted an ad in the paper inviting parents of palsy children to a meeting in Brooklyn. I wasn't keen on going, but she pushed me to go, and I wound up that night as President of the Cerebral Palsy Association, a little group of a dozen or so parents. Our first plan was to raise money for a much needed clinic to provide some services for these youngsters.

... Most important was my meeting Leonard Goldenson, head of Paramount Pictures Theatres at the time. He called out of the blue and asked me to lunch. I had never met him. I had been sending out letters to try to raise funds for the clinic, and he came upon my letter because he and Estelle had a daughter with cerebral palsy. Mrs. Goldenson had had German measles early in her pregnancy. Leonard thought our cause was great, but that we were hampered because our first organization was a local one.

The Goldensons and the Hausmans became the founders of the national organization, United Cerebral Palsy. UCP became a prototype for many other national health organizations devoted to illnesses and handicaps that were unknown except to the hundreds of thousands and perhaps millions who suffered from them.

. . . .

Students at Vanderbilt University in Nashville, Tennessee, formed themselves into a student health coalition to provide health services to one particularly poverty-stricken area of eastern Tennessee. Gradually, they realized that all their time and effort could barely make a dent in the needs of "isolated, impoverished Appalachian communities." The student health coalition became the Center for Health Services, which continues to provide direct services, but more significantly presses successfully for the establishment of public health centers. Despite their impact, succeeding generations of students from Vanderbilt and the many other colleges and universities that joined in the program realized that the people themselves had to become involved in their own health and the factors that influence it.

. . . .

In 1987, Carrie May Reser of Denver received one of the "9 Who Care Awards" from Channel 9, KUSA, for her performance as an exceptional advocate:

> Carrie May Reser of Denver has been a quadriplegic since age 15 when she fell and fractured her neck. Her disability hasn't kept her from becoming a wife, a mother and founder of a nationally known advocacy group. May is now President of D.A.W.S., Diasbled American Workers Security. DAWS, under May's leadership, was instrumental in the enactment of legislation to return benefits to millions of Americans who had been cut from the Social Security rolls without a hearing. She devotes countless hours as an advocate for the disabled and needy.

. . . .

A different type of advocacy effort aimed at the well-being of children is called "Project Amnesty," which received one of the 1986 President's Volunteer Action Awards:

> In 1985, Gloria Allred developed Project Amnesty as a pilot project in five California counties as a way of increasing child support payments. Her efforts were a response to the fact that over two million absent California parents fail to pay an adequate level of child support for their children each year. Because collection of past due support and the development of a regular payment schedule for many of the parents had proven very difficult, many mothers were forced to depend on Aid to Families with Dependent Children support in order to provide adequately for their families.
>
> Project Amnesty provided a period in which parents who were behind in their payments could "catch up" without fear of penalty or jail sentences. To urge parents to pay their court-ordered support, Ms. Allred developed a public awareness campaign that included radio and television public service announcements in both Spanish and English,

posters, bumper stickers and billboards. Because of limited funds, Ms. Allred paid for the production of many of the materials.

When Governor Deukmejian declared the period of June 16 through August 16, 1985, as Child Support Awareness Weeks, Project Amnesty urged parents to bring their support payments up to date during that time. Announcements warned that failure to pay support is a crime and that those who had not paid by the end of the amnesty period were subject to arrest.

The five participating counties each realized an increase in collections ranging from five to twenty-four percent. Total child support collections during the period were up almost two million dollars for an overall increase of more than thirteen and a half percent.

One of the heartening developments arising from those initial efforts occurred when, more than a decade later, there was a National Court Appointed Advocate Association (CASA) with more than 17,000 volunteers operating in 26 states.

. . . .

Advocacy influences all kinds of needs. In a profile entitled "Audubon People" by Ruth Norris in *Audubon Magazine* (September 1981), there are these good descriptions of the diversity and impact of activists:

> They are people who see something that needs to be done and then take it upon themselves to do it. They have been the driving force of the Audubon movement, from George Bird Grinnell, who rallied the readers of *Forest and Stream* to the cause of protecting birds, to Rachel Carson, whose classic *Silent Spring* told the devastating truth about pesticides, to the chapter leaders in every state today who devote their time and talent to keeping air and water clean, preserving wild places, and teaching the values of the natural world. Volunteers like the eleven we present here have proved time and again that one person can make an important difference to the quality of life in a neighborhood, a community, even a much larger area.
>
> Activists, of course, come with a variety of interests and styles. This group is something of a cross section of the

hundreds of dedicated members who carry the Audubon banner in every region of the country. Some are "natural" leaders; others were accidentally, even reluctantly, drawn into the political process. True to the National Audubon Society image, a few are birders who discovered threats to the habitat of a native species. One or two wouldn't recognize anything more esoteric than a robin if it walked up and introduced itself. Their common denominator is a commitment to special places and creatures and to the planet we live on. Together they represent the ways in which that commitment can be expressed.

. . . .

The interest and impact of citizens on their urban environment was described in a May 17, 1988, *Washington Post* story by Roger K. Lewis headed "Citizens Increasingly Active, Savvy in Fighting Battles With Developers." The story said in part:

> First, it's clear that public interest in and awareness of planning and zoning is increasing. People who used to feel powerless or disinterested, if not unaffected, now realize that they can influence the course of growth within their communities. They know more, speak out more, and are willing to invest more time and money, if necessary, to fight for their cause.
> Second, citizen sophistication is greater. Organized grass-roots groups are proliferating like gypsy moths and they know how to "play the game" with government and business organizations. They know how to find and employ experts, how to lobby, how to get publicity. For developers, who used to be concerned primarily with financial, governmental and marketing factors, activist citizens can become another "force majeure" to be reckoned with.

. . . .

To bring their causes to the forefront of public attention some volunteers are willing to engage in civil disobedience and, like Henry David Thoreau, who wrote "Civil Disobedience" more than 125 years ago, are willing to pay the consequences. As recently as October 16, 1988, *The Washington Post* carried a story by Lynne Duke headed "A Campaign of Civil Disobedience" that began, "Activists for the Homeless Face Daily Arrest." The article continued:

> None of the eight housing activists from Seattle had been arrested before, so perhaps it was understandable that they needed advice last week on jail house rules for their trip behind bars in the District.
> "Do they let you keep your hat in jail?" asked Joe Martin, 38.
> "When they take the urine test, do you have to do it in front of somebody?" asked 67-year-old Mary Haggerty.
> Mitch Snyder, of the Community for Creative Non-Violence, which provided food and lodging for the out-of-town protesters, briefed the group on what was in store. The next day, Wednesday, Martin and three others—including a lone Louisville man—lifted their voices in song in the middle of the Rotunda of the U.S. Capitol, illegally breaking the hush maintained by gawking tourists.
> Speaking through a bullhorn, a U.S. Capitol police officer ordered the protesters to cease, and about a dozen members of the Civil Disturbance Unit materialized, in black jumpsuits, surrounding the singers.
> "I ask you to sing along," Martin said to the tourists, who kept silent.
> Still singing "This Land Is Your Land," Martin, Stella Ortega, Wayne Quinn and Louis Valdez Jr. were handcuffed and led away.
> That scene, with variations, has been unfolding every weekday since September 26, when the first wave of protesters from around the nation set out from Snyder's CCNV shelter on Second Street NW on a short march to the Capitol. The protests will continue until Election Day, November 8.
> Daily, the protesters have held a vigil on the West Steps, then carried out an act of civil disobedience designed to focus public attention on the lack of housing for the poor and homeless. Specifically, group members say they want Congress to restore deep cuts in housing programs that have taken place since 1981....
> ... Ortega, affiliated with a social service agency in Seattle called El Centro de la Raza, and Beverly Sims, of Seattle's Emergency Housing Coalition, said that the two-day sojourn to Washington had shown them that their work

on behalf of the poor and the homeless in Seattle is being repeated by others nationwide—that they are not alone.

The name Mother Jones hardly suggests hellfire and revolution, but further examination reveals a woman who was one of the fiercest advocates in American history. In the tenth anniversary issue of the magazine dedicated to and named after her, the editors note that "When Mary Harris Jones was introduced to a college audience as a 'great humanitarian,' she retorted, 'No! I'm a hell raiser!' And so she was. Mother Jones started unions, ran strikes, fought for prison reform, supported revolutions, and spent weeks at a time in jail!"

In 1986, the *Mother Jones* publication initiated an annual series called "Heroes" to recognize "people who showed the same spirit—men and women with the capacity to encourage and inspire, to bring people together, and to work for a more just America." The editors described the winners: "The men and women we profile here lead prosaic lives—working in homeless shelters, organizing the unemployed, gathering petitions—yet they are the connective tissue that binds people together. In a society resistant to change from below, they are persistent, feisty, and courageous. They have organized their communities to fight back, gathered the information government tries to hide, exposed corporate greed in the courts, and comforted the victims of abuse and neglect. These are not the darlings of the powerful. We celebrate them because they challenge power."

. . . .

In the 1980s we are blessed with hundreds of organizations that are run and controlled by volunteers dedicated to securing rights and opportunities for their own populations. They deal with blacks, women, Puerto Ricans, Cubans, Mexicans, and even specific Indian tribes. A prototype is the Native American Rights Fund (NARF), which exists to provide poor and disadvantaged people access to lawyers and the legal process. NARF's executive director, John Echohawk, says:

> For the first time, native Americans are guaranteed quality advocacy for sustained periods to successfully advance their rights. What a difference that knowl-

> edge makes in the legal arena—to our opponents—as well as to native Americans. . . . For the first time, America's Indians are being assured that the white man's system can work for, and not just against them.

. . . .

In 1942, a group of black leaders joined together in what is now known as the Durham Conference, which declared that "compulsory segregation is unjust." Together they set forth the specifics of reforms they considered the most important: "political and civil rights, jobs, education, agriculture, military service, social welfare and health." A year later, the Conference of White Southerners on Race Relations met in Atlanta, agreed with the Durham Statement, and pronounced its objectives just. Three months later, a joint committee from both groups met in Richmond, Virginia, to organize the Southern Regional Council

> . . . for the improvement of economic, civic and race conditions in the South in all efforts toward regional and racial development; to attain through research and action programs the ideals and practices of equal opportunity for all people in the region; to reduce race tension, the basis of racial tension, racial misunderstanding and racial distrust; to develop and integrate leadership in the South on new levels of regional development and fellowship; and to cooperate with local, state and regional agencies on all levels in the attainment of the desired objectives.

The Southern Regional Council had its origins in the Commission on Interracial Cooperation, established in 1919. Principal funding originally came from the Rosenwald Fund and a diverse group of church bodies, labor unions, individuals, and small grants from foundations. In a summary of the council's first thirty years, *The Atlanta Constitution* reported:

> They wanted a regional organization, not from a provincial desire to separate the South's problems from the nation's, but from the conviction that such an organization has unique advantages. It can express the best and often

neglected elements of Southern thought and conscience; it can serve as a convincing demonstration of Southerners working together as fellow citizens, without regard to race, and can tap local resources and initiative often inaccessible to agencies outside the region.

These efforts were, of course, just a prelude to the advocacy and activism that were soon to follow. While earlier groups, like the General Education Board, felt they "must operate within the restraints of segregation," later activists and their founders insisted that empowerment was the liberating stage necessary to enable people to exercise their potential.

The Carnegie Corporation took the lead in support of the Law Students' Civil Rights Research Council and the NAACP Legal Defense and Education Fund/Earl Warren Legal Training Program, which were trying to increase the number of black lawyers in the South. Eli Evans, then a program officer for Carnegie and now president of the Revson Foundation, reports: "Ultimately, 38 foundations and 30 corporations invested $7 million in the same project, which increased the number of (black) students in Southern universities from 22 students in 1969 to 427 seven years later. This became the talent pool for elected officials, university trustees, school board members, etc." A special report entitled "A Step Toward Equal Justice" contained an evaluation of the program and included a case study that began:

> On opposite corners of the intersection of Second Avenue and Ninth Street in Columbus, Georgia, stand two structures, each intentionally functional and unintentionally symbolic. Outwardly, the more impressive of the two is the 11-story Government Center, which houses the only consolidated city-county administration in Georgia. It is so new that the concrete still smells damp. The other, far less prepossessing, is a modest, rambling frame building that once was a notorious local "sporting house." The gold-lettered sign suspended over the door announces "Bishop and Hudlin, Attorneys at Law."
>
> To the 170,000 residents of Muscogee County, the Government Center is a glass-and-concrete embodiment of change. Rising out of a fountain-studded plaza on the site of the late, unlamented old courthouse, the Center soars

> gracefully above a montage of sagging Victorian homes, colorless commercial buildings, and mighty churches.
>
> To Sanford Bishop, 26, and his partner Richard Hudlin, 27, the white frame house opposite is the embodiment of an opportunity. For Bishop and Hudlin are both young, talented and Black, and they have accepted the challenge of proving that Columbus can move into a new era as easily as it moved into a new courthouse.

. . . .

On another front, in 1984, CBS Inc. pledged $1.25 million to the Hispanic Policy Development Project

> ... to support studies on the urgent needs and problems confronting Hispanic communities in the United States; to identify and evaluate policy options for dealing with such specific needs and problems; to communicate the results of these studies to policy and decision makers, the media and the general public; to include broadly representative non-Hispanic and Hispanic leaders in the activities of the organization, in order to increase their involvement and strengthen the impact of the organization's efforts; and to work closely with Hispanic institutions and scholars to build bridges between them, to increase the visibility of Hispanic policy leadership, and to develop opportunities for young Hispanic policy makers and analysts.

Another dimension of empowerment is voter registration. The Stern family, picking up where Mrs. Edgar Stern's father, Julius Rosenwald, left off, has been in the forefront of voter education efforts, beginning in Mrs. Stern's home state of Louisiana. She was a rarity with her early and steadfast support of the unpopular effort to register blacks in the South and minorities throughout the country.

When Lester Dunbar was executive director of the Southern Regional Council, SRC conducted a large Voter Education Project (VEP), which was later spun off and headed by Vernon Jordan before he went on to the United Negro College Fund and the National Urban League. Charles Rooks, now head of the Fred Meyer Charitable Trust, worked with VEP and said:

> While the "revolution" in Southern politics caused by the emergence of Black political power is due to many factors, the role of the Voter Education Project (earlier a project of the Southern Regional Council) is an important part of this story. Ford, Rockefeller Brothers, Carnegie, and some other large foundations made important contributions, but the real "heroes" in the foundation world were a group of small foundations (Taconic, Norman, etc.) that supported VEP at the outset, when it was a much riskier undertaking.

The need for greater attention to women's issues was highlighted by a 1985 survey on the worldwide state of women issued to coincide with the United Nation's International Decade for Women. According to the May 1985 Newsletter of the Council on Foundations, the survey concludes:

> Whether in the economy, education, health, or government, there is no major field of activity in any country in which women have attained equality with men. . . . [T]he influx of women into the paid labor force has not significantly narrowed the gap between men's and women's pay; nor has it stemmed the rising tide of poverty among women. Despite the key role that women have in third world economies, they have been largely bypassed in development strategies.

One of the increasing number of organizations that devotes all its attention to women's issues is the Women's Foundation, which states its mission thusly: "For the fulfillment of the many dreams and aspirations of young girls and for the continued strengthening and empowerment of all women." To achieve this mission, the Women's Foundation has funded such diverse programs as the Alliance Against Women's Oppression, Big Sisters, the California Coordinating Council for Domestic Violence, the Children's Council of San Francisco, the Comparable

Worth Project, the Displaced Homemakers Center, the San Mateo Advisory Council on Women, the Shasta County Women's Refuge, Stepping Stone Growth Center, Women Against Violence-Emergency Services (WAVES)/Advocates for Women, Womenspace Unlimited, and Women's Voices.

. . . .

The needs and aspirations of minorities, women, and others have frequently been the focus of "alternative funds," a newer phenomenon in philanthropy. These funds have been springing up in many communities and regions. The July/August 1984 issue of *Foundation News* carried a feature on alternative funds, which, it says, were initially called "change-oriented" or "radical" funds. The article quotes David Hunter of the Stern Fund as follows:

> . . . [T]he alternatives share a firm commitment to a redistribution of wealth and power. They're all concerned with furthering democracy in American society; and economic democracy—widespread participation in the economy—may well be the tripping point. They do not believe, as the more conservative foundations do, that the goal is simply to train [the] underprivileged so they can get a piece of the action. The goal is to change the action itself.

The article's author, Roger M. Williams, adds: "If that is the goal, the method is grassroots 'empowerment,' a Sixties phrase that means enabling the most downtrodden of Americans to 'gain control over their own lives.'"

. . . .

8
Don't Save Me From the Left or Right

FROM TWO EXTREMES, people who believe passionately in freedom are calling for increased regulations to restrict what their opposites can do.

With the growing influence of conservative evangelical churches, liberals are calling for revision of the laws that define what a religion is and what religions can't do. From their side, influential conservatives are promoting legal schemes to "defund the left," to limit the outreach of organizations like Planned Parenthood that deal with causes they consider dangerous to the country.

Liberals, who for fifty years have been listening to their Roman Catholic priests tell them how to vote, or who still hear their black preachers endorse candidates, or who encouraged their Lutheran ministers to march in Selma, want to clamp down on what can be done in the name of religion. Conservatives, who

---

"Opinion" column in *The Christian Science Monitor,* December 28, 1983.

preach faith in people, minimal government, and clearer separation of church and state, want expansion of governmental control over what they define as unholy.

If both sides get their way, we'll have more laws to protect us from the right and the left—and less freedom for everyone.

Out of passion and bitterness, both sides are losing sight of the protection of the larger freedoms of speech and assembly, and of their wide-open opportunities to spread what they consider the truth. Any infringement on these freedoms and opportunities will sooner or later infringe both of them and all of us.

If some people believe that the rest of us must be protected from certain extreme ideas, or if they're frightened that we won't make the right decisions for ourselves, our families, and our communities, there is comfort in Thomas Jefferson's advice: "I know of no safe depository of the ultimate powers of society but the people themselves; and if we think them not enlightened enough to exercise their control with a wholesome discretion, the remedy is not to take it from them, but to inform their discretion by education."

Norman Lear started People for the American Way to warn people of the seductive media campaigns of the Moral Majority, and if Lear goes too far, someone else will come along to correct him. Along the way, the people learn and grow.

There are some causes in the land that I believe are downright dangerous, and there are situations where opposing crusades spend staggering amounts only to achieve a standoff. Our protection—and theirs—is in our right to disclose what we know, not to foreclose what they do.

If some groups clearly trespass the law, the authority is already at hand to deal with them. Hopefully, though, the law will not be administered with a heavy hand. Democracy and I can survive my priest telling me how to vote on a candidate who supports federal appropriations for abortions, but we will not survive if he can be too easily silenced on public issues, or if true believers in any cause can legally stifle their doubters.

What Voluntary Activity Can and Cannot Do for America

WITH HIS EMPHASIS on private-sector initiatives, President Reagan provided welcome attention to voluntary organizations and to personal responsibility for community service, but along the way he contributed to an exaggerated notion of what voluntary activity can do and what government need not do. President Bush intends to expand the encouragement of personal service through stimulation of the "thousand points of light," which can be a great boon to active citizenship but only if he learns the lessons from his predecessor's miscalculations.

A large part the misunderstanding concerning the role and capacity of nonprofit activity stems from limited research and data on the sector. America's pluralism and generosity have been

---

Excerpts from an article of the same title that appeared in the September/October 1989 issue of *Public Administration Review*.

so natural that there never seemed a need to study them. Now that misinformation is skewing public policies and perceptions, there is a scramble to sort out what the voluntary sector is really all about and what the differences are between government and nonprofits. Much of the research is producing a body of knowledge about what the independent or voluntary sector is and what it is not, and both views are proving vital in sorting out its usefulness and limitations.

On the plus side, this third sector of activity and organizations provides a different way of seeing and doing things. For example, foreign visitors who come to learn about American philanthropic and voluntary activity report that a very real aspect of freedom and influence is missing without this buffer sector. At best, they find it restrictive and at worst oppressive when only one governmental system exists for education, culture, or religion, and where there is no tradition of independent service and criticism.

Though the size of this sector in the United States is smaller than most people assume and far smaller than government, it is impressive nevertheless. Approximately 900,000 exempt organizations are officially registered with the Internal Revenue Service, but that does not count religious congregations or the local affiliates of many national organizations such as the Boy Scouts and American Cancer Society. When these and all the less formal neighborhood and community groups are added in, the figure is something over two million.

In terms of personal participation, a 1988 report from INDEPENDENT SECTOR, "Giving and Volunteering in the United States,"[1] points out that individuals represent approximately 90 percent of all giving. Corporate giving, as important as it is, only represents 5 percent, as does foundation giving. The base of personal participation of both giving and volunteering is enormously broad and growing. Three-fourths of American families are contributors, giving an average of $790 a year to the causes of their choice. Approximately half of all adult Americans are active volunteers, and they give an average of 4.7 hours a week. Twenty million Americans give 5 percent or more of their income to charity, and 23 million volunteer five or more hours a week. Contributions to voluntary organizations exceeded $100 billion in 1988, and 80 million people volunteered a total of 14.9 billion hours, which, conservatively estimated, is worth another $150 billion.*

One need not go back in American history to find examples of all this caring. A far larger proportion and many more parts of the population are involved in community activities today than at any time in history. Americans organize to influence every conceivable aspect of the human condition and are willing to stand up and be counted on almost any public issue. In recent times, Americans have successfully organized to deal with a vast array of human needs and aspirations, including the rights of women, learning disabilities, conflict resolution, Hispanic culture and rights, the aged, voter registration, Native Americans, experimental theater, international understanding, drunk driving, population control, consumerism, and on and on. Volunteers' interests and impact extend from neighborhoods to the ozone layer and beyond.

Beyond the urgent causes and crusades, the independent sector simply provides more people a chance to do their "own thing"—to be different—to be a bit freer—to be unique. In an INDEPENDENT SECTOR Occasional Paper based on his book *The Endangered Sector*, Waldemar Nielsen summarized the wonderful variety of interests that Americans freely pursue through voluntary organizations. Here are some examples:

> If your interest is people, you can help the elderly by a contribution to the Grey Panthers; or teenagers through the Jean Teen Scene of Chicago; or young children through your local nursery school; or everyone by giving to the Rock of All Ages in Philadelphia.
> If your interest is animals, there is the ASPCA and Adopt-a-Pet; if fishes, the Izaak Walton League; if birds, the American Homing Pigeon Institute or the Easter Bird Banding Association.
> If you are interested in tradition and social continuity, there is the Society for the Preservation of Historic Landmarks and the Portland Friends of Cast Iron Architecture; if social change is your passion, there is Common Cause;

---

*For figures as of 1992, please see Chapter 1, "Origins, Dimensions, and Impact of America's Voluntary Spirit."

and, if that seems too sober for you, there is the Union of Radical Political Economists or perhaps the Theatre for Revolutionary Satire.

If your pleasure is music, there is a supermarket of choices—from Vocal Jazz to the Philharmonic Society to the American Guild of English Hand Bellringers.

If you don't know quite what you want, there is Get Your Head Together, Inc. of Glen Ridge, New Jersey. If your interests are contradictory, there is the Great Silence Broadcasting Foundation of California. If they are ambiguous, there is the Tombstone Health Service of Arizona.[2]

One of the largest roles of voluntary organizations is religious expression and protection of that freedom. In "From Belief to Commitment,"[3] a 1988 INDEPENDENT SECTOR report based on the largest study ever undertaken of the community service role of religious congregations, extensive documentation shows that religious congregations are the primary service providers for neighborhoods. It is my experience that the poorer the community, the larger that role and impact. Beyond the exercise of religious freedom and the community services provided by religious congregations, these institutions have been and continue to be the places where many moral issues are raised and pursued. In his mid-nineteenth century observations on the American scene, Alexis de Tocqueville saw this country's network of voluntary organizations not so much as service providers but as "the moral associations" where such values as charity and responsibility to others were taught and where the nation's crusades took root.[4]

I am constantly aware of how much the country's patterns of community service and advocacy relate to the earliest activities of churches as well as to the initial and continuing protection of freedom of religion. Despite how obvious this is, people tend to set aside this whole half of the voluntary sector as though it does not really belong, relating largely to salvation, but if one looks at what the conscience, the meeting ground, and the organized neighborliness represented by religious congregations mean to the kind of society America is, religion takes on a different and larger significance.

In the composite then, an almost dizzying array of activity exists. Americans inform, protest, assist, teach, heal, build, advocate, comfort, testify, support, solicit, canvas, demonstrate, guide, feed, criticize, organize, appeal, usher, contribute, and in a hundred other ways serve people and causes. In the face of all this activity, some people decry what they think of as uncoordinated, frenetic do-goodism. Most, however, including President Bush, see it as the thousand or million points of light that give all people a chance to serve, have influence, and "do their own thing."

When focusing only on the positive contributions of the sector, it is possible to get carried away with its importance. Many champions of philanthropy consider it to be America's greatest set of institutions, and they are critical that I refer to it as an extra dimension. One needs, however, to be cautious about putting this sector ahead of other aspects of the democratic way of life. It is important to remember the basic values of American society: freedom; the worth and dignity of the individual; equal opportunity; justice; and mutual responsibility. The fundamental vehicles for preserving and enhancing those basic values are representative government, starting with one person, one vote; the freedoms of religion, speech, and assembly; a free press; a system of justice based on due process and presumption of innocence; and universal public education. Philanthropy and voluntary action help to preserve and enhance those values, but they do not transcend them.

It is useful to realize that the independent sector is much smaller than the government and commercial sectors. In terms of national income, commerce totals 79 percent, government is 15 percent, and the whole of the independent sector is only 6 percent. The comparison becomes even starker when one measures the total expenditures of nonprofit organizations against the expenditures of government. Nonprofit groups spend approximately $250 billion a year, as contrasted with the combined expenditures of the three levels of government, which comes to about $2.5 trillion.[5] Thus, the ratio is about one to ten. It should also be noted that approximately one-third of the income of the nonprofits comes from governmental allocations.

When seen this way, it becomes clearer that the sector is small compared to government and that all such private efforts have to be targeted uniquely or they will not be worth much measured against society's needs and aspirations. There are ways by which that 10 percent can be spent to make a difference far beyond its relative size, but if the funds are not targeted carefully, they add only an incidental rather than an extra dimension. Further, if a large part of the nonprofits' 10 percent is diverted to cover what government no longer feels it can do, these organizations lose their capacity to be different from government.

A few years ago I attended a Ditchley Foundation conference in England on the future of philanthropy in the Western world. It became clear that, for other countries, the total amounts represented by philanthropy and voluntary action are minuscule compared to what government spends. In Britain, the total voluntary sector is about 2 percent the size of government, compared with America's 10 percent. Even at that, representatives from other countries argued that the sector provides vital elements of flexibility, innovation, creativity, and criticism, and that it must be preserved.

One of the issues discussed was whether philanthropic dollars should be used to supplement government expenditures, particularly at a time of government cutbacks. At that stage both Prime Minister Thatcher and President Reagan were arguing that private philanthropy should be used to make up for government retrenchment, and many U.S. mayors were urging foundations and corporations to help keep schools, libraries, and parks open and to maintain other public services. It became clear that while philanthropy has a responsibility to deal with emergency matters, particularly those involving human suffering, in the long run the small amount that philanthropy represents must be reserved for unique extra purposes such as flexibility and criticism, or it may not be worth preserving at all.

Another limitation involves the arbitrary focus of most contributors and voluntary organizations. These groups are not responsible for the general welfare. People target their contributions to organizations that deal with the Lutheran elderly, Catholic schools, or Oriental art; or contributors and organizations are focused on assistance to a particular neighborhood, population, or country. It is not in the cards—and should not be—that government has the capacity to change the practice of people giving to the causes of their choice as long as those causes are represented by legitimate organizations.

This relates to another limitation, involving accountability. Voluntary organizations must certainly be accountable for proper use of all sources of income and make full disclosure of their finances, but they are not solely accountable to government, and to make them so would eliminate the very flexibility and independence that comprise their principal value to society.

An additional limitation involves the role of nonprofit organizations to protect and extend freedom and rights rather than being simply a network of nonprofit service agencies. Some mayors, governors, and presidents see or want to see voluntary organizations as deliverers of services, and they are generally antagonized when these organizations behave as gadflies or, worse, as critics. In every administration starting with President Nixon's, there have been serious proposals to strip or limit tax exemption and deduction for organizations that do not devote a large proportion of their activities to direct services to the disadvantaged, and to strip altogether the nonprofit status of organizations that emphasize activism and advocacy. It is surely a maddening thing to those responsible for providing services that so many nonprofit organizations seem to be preoccupied with public policies. For public officials, this is a decided drawback to voluntary organizations, but in the long run it is the quintessential role and contribution of the nonprofit sector.

Against this backdrop, it is not altogether surprising that President Reagan had serious misconceptions about the role and capacities of voluntary organizations. Indeed, it is instructive that we had a President who was committed to strengthening voluntary initiative but who ended up doing much the opposite. Though some attribute this to disingenuousness, it was more likely a result of a genuine misunderstanding of what voluntary organizations can and cannot do for America. A painful but useful lesson of those years involves a more realistic understanding of what responsibilities cannot be transferred from government to the voluntary sector.

President Reagan did devote a good deal of attention to the activities of nonprofit groups, including honoring private-sector initiatives by individuals, organizations, and corporations. To the extent that a society is what it venerates, Reagan's efforts in that area were very helpful and will have lasting benefits. Those advantages, however, were more than counterbalanced by many of the Reagan Administration's other actions, which undermined the ability of voluntary organizations to fulfill the larger role that the President expected of them. The difficulties began with a basic misunderstanding of the size and role of the voluntary sector. The President pushed these groups to assume more responsibility than they could practically handle. As a result, many of them, particularly those dealing with the most vulnerable, faced intolerable expectations and ended up with a good deal of undeserved guilt and blame.

From the start of that administration, I was struck by how little those who were attempting to foster philanthropy and voluntary action really understood it. Within months of the inauguration, I found myself working with White House staff and volunteers newly involved with the President's Task Force on Private Initiatives who really believed that corporate philanthropy alone, which then totalled only $3 billion (or a fraction of 1 percent of the federal budget), could take over support of programs utterly beyond anything that corporate philanthropy could ever achieve. There was a total lack of understanding of the size of private giving. These were not people who were trying to find an excuse to cut public programs, but they were officials who genuinely believed that private philanthropy and voluntary organizations were far larger than is in fact the case.

The Reagan Administration's second mistake involved an unintended but serious undercutting of the income of many voluntary organizations. As indicated earlier, more than one-third of the income of the voluntary sector is contracted by government to such nonprofit groups as job-training centers, homes for the aged, and research universities. A significant and disproportionate share of the government's budget cuts came out of the income of its voluntary partners.

Simultaneously, several changes in the 1986 Tax Act undercut the ability of many voluntary groups to keep up with prior rates of fundraising growth. For the first full year following the tax changes, the rate of increased giving by individuals dropped 50 percent, just as the administration had been warned it would.

To compound the income problem, the Reagan Administration, which had forced most nonprofits to scramble for new and higher levels of noncontributed and nongovernmental support, tried to tax previously exempt categories of other income such as fees, sales, and interest.

There were, as well, repeated efforts by the Reagan Administration to curb the advocacy activities of voluntary organizations. Office of Management and Budget proposals would have stripped from voluntary organizations that receive any government funding almost all their rights to engage simultaneously in representations before government. Similarly, proposed Internal Revenue Service regulations would have restricted greatly the advocacy rights of all tax-exempt organizations. In short, there was an attitude that voluntary service was to be applauded and advocacy to be discouraged. This ignored the reality that much of the best voluntary effort in U.S. history involved those who advocated for many of the public policies and programs in which Americans take pride today.

In the composite, the voluntary organizations that President Reagan wanted to help were in fact faced with increased expectations, decreased government support, an undercutting of their ability to raise new money, the prospect of new taxes, and a challenge to their advocacy role.

. . . .

The 1920s were an earlier high point for the visibility and appreciation of voluntary activity. World War I produced a wave of civic participation, and the 1920s were "can do" years. With the advent of the Depression, President Hoover, who had achieved national prominence and leadership through national and international philanthropic endeavors such as the Commission for the Relief of Belgium, called upon American generosity and voluntary effort to expand to meet escalating needs. When the voluntary sector could not, there was a sense that it let the country down, and when government failed to move into the void, the public wondered if anybody cared.

Classical Marxist theory held that allowing other systems to exist, including free enterprise and voluntary organizations, obscured the absolute role and responsibility of government. This philosophy overlooked the greater advantages of pluralistic problem solving, maximum citizen involvement, and liberating outlets for creativity and fulfillment, but in the continuing confusion between the relative roles of government and philanthropy, the old Marxist argument cannot be dismissed altogether. Those who believe in the superiority of a three-sector society bear a particular burden to be sure that support for free enterprise and voluntarism does not in fact obscure the role and responsibility of government. In 1932, Rheinhold Niebuhr, hardly a Marxist, summarized the immediate situation: "[T]he effort to try to make voluntary charity solve the problem of major social crises . . . results only in monumental hypocrisies. . . ."[6]

During the 1930s and throughout the war and postwar 1940s and 1950s, the focus in the United States was necessarily on the responsibilities and capacities of government. Gradually, however, people of all political and philosophical viewpoints began to realize the practical limitations of big government as well as the importance of an active citizenry in helping to make government an effective provider of options and alternatives. This eventually led to the explosion in number and impact of voluntary organizations from the 1960s through the 1980s and to a denigration of government for its limitations and shortcomings.

The essential lesson taught by the 1920s and Herbert Hoover is that Americans need both strong government and a strong voluntary sector and that they will not have either if national leaders do not understand the relative roles of the two. Voluntary organizations provide wonderful elements of spirit, participation, service, influence, and the freedom to do one's own "thing," but if government overloads them with the basic responsibility for public services, undercuts their income, and limits their freedom to advocate and criticize, they will fail society and America will find itself at another point of national breakdown, with people demanding that government do it all. That can be avoided if Americans understand the parallel lessons of the 1930s and 1980s: Voluntary groups can make government more responsible and efficient, serve as vehicles for influence and empowerment, and provide opportunities for pluralistic problem solving, but they cannot take the place of government. Officials must understand that, when it comes to abject interdependence, it is to democratic government that Americans rightfully turn for representation.

Although America's voluntary sector should not be viewed as more than an extra dimension, it represents very special opportunities for people to have influence and choices. Efforts by all Americans, including President Bush and Congress, should be devoted to building upon that uniqueness without exaggerating what the sector can do or what government should not do.

Notes

1. Virginia Hodgkinson and Murray Weitzman, "Giving and Volunteering in the United States." Washington, D.C.: INDEPENDENT SECTOR, 1988.

2. Waldemar Nielsen, "The Third Sector: Keystone of a Caring Society," Occasional Paper. Washington, D.C.: INDEPENDENT SECTOR, 1980.

3. Virginia Hodgkinson, Murray Weitzman, and Arthur Kirsch, "From Belief to Commitment." Washington, D.C.: INDEPENDENT SECTOR, 1988.

4. Alexis de Tocqueville, "Of the Use Which Americans Make of Public Associations in Civil Life," in *Democracy in America*, vol. 2, book 2, chapter 5. New York: Alfred A. Knopf, Borzoi Books, 1976.

5. Virginia Hodgkinson and Murray Weitzman, *Dimensions of the Independent Sector: A Statistical Profile*, 2d ed. Washington, D.C.: INDEPENDENT SECTOR, 1986.

6. Rhinehold Niebuhr, *Contributions of Religion to Social Work*. New York: Columbia University Press, 1932. p. 29.

10

State of the Sector: With Particular Attention to Its Independence

THERE ARE MANY ROLES that philanthropy and voluntary effort fulfill, but their central value is the *extra* dimension they provide for doing and seeing things differently. They cannot take the place of government, but they do provide additional ways to address our needs, pursue our hopes, and help keep government responsive and effective.

. . . .

At the heart of the uniqueness of the sector is its relative independence and freedom to contribute to innovation, advocacy, criticism, and, where necessary, reform. With this freedom, the

---

Excerpts from a paper of the same title prepared at the request of the INDEPENDENT SECTOR Annual Meeting Planning Committee for discussion at the Annual Meeting and Assembly of Members, October 1987, Washington, D.C.

sector has provided an enormously important extra dimension in our pursuit of happiness and the protection of inalienable rights. Its impact is clear in just about every field of endeavor, including fields as different as architecture, health, human rights, historic preservation, international understanding, the arts, neighborhood improvement, empowerment, patriotism, agriculture, rocketry, physics, the homeless, and astronomy. Most of the great movements of our society have had their origins in the independent sector: abolition of slavery, clarification and protection of civil rights, creation of public libraries, care and opportunities for the handicapped, and on and on. Some who led those efforts were viewed as unpopular, troublesome, rabble-rousing, and perhaps even dangerous. It has been one of the hallmarks of the sector that it has offered support for unpopular people and ideas and protected their freedom.

Henry Allen Moe, longtime head of the John Simon Guggenheim Memorial Foundation, delivered the Founders Day Address at Johns Hopkins University in 1951 and gave it an appropriate title: "The Power of Freedom." He spoke of the genius of America—its freedom as a society and the freedom it allows individuals and institutions to be different. He quoted Elihu Root: "Freedom is the supreme treasure of our country." And he quoted Detlev Bronk: "Freedom is the grand ingredient of the great adventures of the human mind."

Occasionally, philanthropic support of unpopular ideas has led government officials and others to question the relative value of the sector's independence versus the need for public control over private expenditure of tax-free dollars. In 1953, the House Select Committee to Investigate Foundations and Other Organizations, popularly known as the Reece Committee, held hearings on the use of foundation grants "for subversive purposes or for active political propaganda." During those hearings, *The Christian Century* published an editorial that presented a convincing argument for preserving philanthropy's independence:

> The central issue then is freedom. The foundations are not prepared to surrender to government the exclusive right to be concerned over the health, the education, the prosperity or even the safety of the people. They should be supported in their liberty to explore social questions. They

State of the Sector: With Particular Attention to Its Independence 81

uphold and practice freedom of enterprise in humanitarian concern for welfare, in intellectual concern for study and research. Having no faith in ignorance as a servant of democracy, they encourage independent inquiry and publication in politics and economics. Knowing that the more important issues, including survival, depend on right national and international relationships, they dig for and disseminate knowledge in these bitterly contested fields.

The historian Merle Curti, writing on "Tradition and Innovation in American Philanthropy: Growth and Present Status of American Foundations" (in the 1961 *Proceedings of the American Philosophical Society*), emphasized that the value of foundations and those they support is their freedom to be creative and that creativity is the quintessential characteristic of nonprofit endeavor:

> This brief account of the way in which American philanthropy has developed from its Old World origins, of the newer methods and agencies that have been adopted or further developed in the United States, and of the kind of private contributions that have been made in various fields has done scant justice to the dedicated work of many individuals and foundations. But it at least suggests the scope and character of what has been done. And it gives support to the thesis that, whatever its limitations, private philanthropy has played a telling part especially in the America of the last seventy-five years in opening the way to a larger emphasis on the esthetic and civic components in the national life. In these respects, in the role that many donors and some foundations have played, and in the distinctive relationships with government that have developed, American philanthropy has a record that is genuinely creative.

. . . .

One of the unanticipated roles of INDEPENDENT SECTOR has turned out to be as a resource for representatives from other countries who are eager to learn more about our philanthropy and voluntary action. They are not people necessarily unhappy with their political structures, but they are keenly aware that a very real aspect of freedom and influence is missing when there isn't a third, or buffer, sector. At best, they find it restrictive and at worst oppressive when there is only the one governmental system for education or health and no tradition of independent service and criticism.

One visitor from a traditionally autocratic country saw value in developing a third sector and figured that the government should just set it up and finance it. When I explained that this would limit the sector's degree of autonomy and thereby the real interest of people in participating, the emissary decided his rulers didn't really want *that* much independence!

I have been serving as a consultant to Israel, which wants to develop its independent sector. In America, we generally ascribe our traditions of pluralism and generosity to the Judaeo-Christian ethic, and thus it is curious that the Jewish homeland should turn to America for advice in developing the voluntary tradition. Understandably, Israel has been preoccupied with building its infrastructure for defense, roads, education, housing, and other pressing needs, but not many of its leaders, in or out of government, realize that something is missing. There are many voluntary organizations, but most of them are almost entirely funded by government and therefore are really more quasi-governmental than voluntary. Almost all contributions come from outside the country. For these reasons and others, there is no vibrant and truly *independent* sector in Isaraei. They now realize that there is something basic missing in not having an additional tier of planners, doers, and critics. To try to stimulate such endeavors, an organization patterned after INDEPENDENT SECTOR has been formed.

. . . .

The traditions of service and reform in the U.S. have now spread to every corner of the population and country, which is decidedly good news. The bad news is that all this perceived rabble-rousing and turmoil are making a lot of people, including government officials, uncomfortable. Part of their understandable response is to want to more narrowly define what is acceptable and, therefore, what is unacceptable public behavior. That might lead to a more orderly society, which may sound pleasantly harmonious, but only until it is one's own outrage that is muted.

Within the larger message that the sector is alive and well, and without contributing to an impression that we are under siege, it is important to indicate some challenges to the future independence of philanthropic and voluntary activity. In order to do this reasonably briefly, I'll no doubt be using some jargon and shorthand, but I hope the basic information will come through.

Examples of Problems

Challenges to Advocacy Rights

Perhaps the epitome of jargon is "OMB A-122," but veterans of the battle of '85 will recognize it instantly. The Office of Management and Budget (OMB) proposed to change the conditions contained in Circular A-122, which governs many of the contractual relationships between the federal government and voluntary organizations. Those changes would have stripped from voluntary organizations that receive any government funding almost all their rights to simultaneously engage in advocacy or even representations before government. Though those regulations were largely defeated, much of the same intent and language reappeared in 1987 in proposed IRS regulations governing the advocacy rights of all tax-exempt organizations. Thanks to a massive effort, those newer proposals have also been defeated, but they may come forward again.

Over the past twelve or more years, the IRS has several times attempted to change the voter education rights of exempt organizations, trying particularly to remove or reduce the current right of voluntary organizations to publish the voting records of legislators on matters of concern to the members of those organizations. Also, the Office of Personnel and Management has been engaged in persistent efforts, often blocked in the courts and Congress, to exclude advocacy organizations from the Combined Federal Campaign, the annual fundraising appeal among federal employees.

These are just three examples of growing challenges to the advocacy role and rights of philanthropic and voluntary organizations. There is a general sense that the institutions of the sector are on more appropriate ground when they are providing services, especially services to the poor, and that it is a questionable extension of tax exemption when such organizations use the privilege of their government-granted tax-free status to turn around and try to influence that same government.

Changes in Other Rules Governing Tax Exemption

Several states are entertaining amendments to their laws governing property tax and other exemptions for nonprofit organizations. Washington, D.C., for example, wanted to allow exemption only for organizations that devote at least 50 percent of their resources to direct services to D.C. residents. Pennsylvania is considering allowing exemption only for voluntary organizations that devote the majority of their resources to those below the poverty line. New York City wanted to limit exemption to educational institutions that provided actual classroom instruction.

In various recent hearings, Congress has considered changes that would have narrowed the definition of who can receive exemption and what can be done with it, usually focusing on advocacy organizations.

A Growing Pattern of Regulation

More and more states and municipalities are developing regulations governing who can march, petition, and raise funds, as well as under what conditions. All this is done in the name of protection of the people, but in the composite these regulations provide overriding opportunities to limit the participation of certain groups. In Schaumburg v. Citizens for a Better Environment, the village leaders adopted an ordinance denying fundraising solicitation rights to organizations with fundraising costs that exceeded 25 percent. On the surface that seemed reasonable, but it ignored the reality of fundraising costs for new organizations as well as for groups dealing with unpopular causes. In the Schaumburg case, the law was imposed on a group that was taking the village leaders to task on environmental issues. IS was able to get many of the country's most prestigious charitable organizations involved in the appeal, so that the issue would not be seen as an isolated instance involving only a weak advocacy organization. Fortunately the Supreme Court supported our position. Our brief called for full disclosure of fundraising costs so that the public could know them, but it argued against foreclosure of an organization's fundraising rights based only on those costs.

In the report of the organizing committee that created INDEPENDENT SECTOR, matters of growing regulation were highlighted.

> There is a pattern of rapidly emerging government regulation of philanthropy and independent organizations. Federal reporting mechanisms and requirements are periodically tightened and new proposals would give the IRS, Post Office Department, Federal Trade Commission and other federal agencies far greater authority over tax-exempt organizations. Not only are disclosure requirements becoming more pronounced, but so too are the opportunities for governmental penalties and even foreclosure.
>
> Thirty-five states and the District of Columbia now have laws governing charitable solicitations and many communities have developed their own ordinances dealing with fund raising, demonstrations and other forms of community action. For example, in Illinois there is a comprehensive state statute requiring annual filing and at least 38 different local laws, each requiring licensing of organizations raising funds locally.
>
> Much of this regulation and oversight are of course initiated to protect people and some of it is brought on by frauds perpetrated in the name of charity, but much of the regulation tends to define what is acceptable organizational behavior, and it is that which is most unacceptable. The nature of much of the regulation and the nightmare complexity and patchwork of it threaten to inhibit the freedoms of speech, assembly and petition.
>
> It is the emerging or unpopular organizations which are particularly at the mercy of all this regulation. The statutes are often unknown to new groups or beyond their capacity to satisfy, and some of the regulations are inherently antagonistic to the kind of activist groups which threaten the status quo. This gives public officials unwarranted authority to limit the activities of such groups, particularly if the new

groups are antagonistic to the officials. There is no greater danger to the preservation of our free society than giving the powers that be any great control over who their own reformers might be.

Limitations on Deductions of Contributions

Recent changes in the tax code underscore the official attitude toward deduction of contributions. Historically, tax policy has recognized the importance of personal contributions and has encouraged deducting gifts from taxable income. This has provided an additional incentive for giving, but more importantly has served to remind all of us that it is the philosophy and policy of the people and our government that giving is a public good which is to be fostered.

Recent loss of the deduction for non-itemizers (those who use the short form) threatens the democratization of giving and ignores the increasing expectations that both government and the people have placed on voluntary organizations. The marked decrease in the proportion of taxpayers who itemize their deductions has also reinforced the belief that deductions, including those for charity, are simply loopholes for the rich. Giving is not a loophole. As we move toward fewer and fewer taxpayers itemizing deductions, we will move toward greater challenges to the deduction mechanism itself.

The Concept of "Tax Expenditures"

There are an increasing number of government officials who argue that because the government loses tax revenue when people deduct gifts from their taxable income, this money is really a tax expenditure and therefore government should have more control over where that money is channeled and how it is spent. The genius of the proposition that people should be free to support the causes of their choice and that government should do everything possible to encourage this aspect of pluralism is being subordinated to simplicity and a strict line of governmental authority.

Proposed Taxes on Exempt Organizations

The House Ways and Means and Senate Finance Committees recently held hearings in which a new five percent tax on the investments and other noncontributed sources of income of foundations and voluntary organizations was considered. In our testimony we said:

> ... this excise tax is contrary to the underlying concept of tax-free organizations. In 1969, Congress imposed a four- percent excise tax on foundations under the rationale and assurances that the income would be used only to monitor the work of foundations. That tax was reduced in 1979 to two percent but still produces $217 million a year (1986), which is six times the total budget of the entire exempt division of IRS. To begin to tax tax-exempt public charities and the foundations that help support them is fundamentally a contradiction.

Concerns About "Competition" Between Businesses and Voluntary Organizations

At a time when contributors, especially corporations, are urging voluntary organizations to be more self-sufficient and entrepreneurial, there are claims of interference with profit-making organizations. Up to now the sector has been on the defensive because the general impression has been that voluntary organizations are moving into territory traditionally occupied by free enterprise. Several examinations now indicate that the opposite is really the case. As third-party payments and other government funding have made some areas, such as alcoholism treatment programs, more attractive for profit-making groups, these businesses have understandably moved to take advantage of the situation.

Though we cannot assume that all the purported overlap is real or unhealthy, neither can we assume that voluntary organizations should serve only the poor and should not charge fees for those who want and can pay for services.

So far the federal government and states that have examined the issue seem inclined to want to find ways to limit the role of voluntary groups.

As with most matters, the dilemma is not altogether new and we can learn something from history. In Massachusetts, in the mid-1850s, there was enormous confusion, competition, and contentiousness among the three sectors as to which should be assigned the running of human-service institutions. It will sound familiar that business advocates felt they could perform many of these functions better and cheaper and that government officials questioned the legitimacy of nonprofit organizations to perform government services. These two ganged up on what they thought was the weaker voluntary sector. They even challenged the very notion of tax exemption for all but church organizations. The matter was settled in 1873, with the principle beautifully articulated by Charles W. Eliot: "The reason for treating these institutions in an exceptional manner is that . . . they contribute to the welfare of the State. Their function is largely a public function; their work is done, primarily indeed, for individuals, but ultimately for the public good. . . ."

Reconsiderations of Unrelated Business Income

Related to the competition issue but not totally subsumed under it are current reexaminations of the unrelated business income tax (UBIT). Current law allows a tax-exempt organization to engage in profit-making ventures but also states that when these ventures are not related to the central mission of the organization, taxes must be paid on the profits.

There are a growing number of administrative and court rulings that narrow the definition of relatedness and therefore require more types and sources of income to be taxed. There are now serious arguments that nonprofit organizations should not be allowed to generate unrelated business income or that the proportion of such income to overall revenue should be greatly restricted.

Dependence on Government Funding

Events of the past eight years, such as the federal government's efforts to restrict the advocacy rights of voluntary groups that accept government funds, accentuate the problem of "greater dependence on government grants, contracts, and other government funds," as pointed up by the IS organizing committee in 1979.

> Many independent organizations increasingly use and seek government funds for their activities. This creates problems of dependence for the individual institutions and reduces the ability of these organizations to function as totally independent organizations. In his essay "The Third Sector," John D. Rockefeller 3rd pointed out that "If government support becomes too large a proportion of a nonprofit institution's budget, it will soon lose its independence and become a de facto government institution."

The Preoccupation of Researchers With the Sector's Service Role

There has been a welcome increase in attention paid to the sector by researchers. However, one real drawback to this attention is how much of it has focused on the service side of the sector. In part, this is an understandable reflection of the fact that data is generally not available on religious institutions, as well as the sense that such institutions are not really the same as hospitals, colleges, museums, and other nonprofit institutions and, therefore, should be excluded so as not to mix apples and oranges. Figures are also not generally available for advocacy and mutual-help organizations, and what is known tells us that the dollars and employees are relatively few compared to the service organizations and therefore not essential to the total figures. The result is that researchers turn to the services, where figures are available and the dollars are significant, and with this "critical mass" before them conduct their studies and draw their conclusions. Obviously, the problem is that the conclusions are assumed to reflect roles, trends, impact, et cetera for the total sector that may not be accurate. They also accentuate direct services as the primary function of the sector, further obscuring the importance of its other functions, particularly religious expression and advocacy.

The above listing is incomplete, but it is probably sufficient to make the case that, at least in the composite, such problems interfere with the perception and protection of independence as the primary role of the independent sector. These problems are compounded by the more general issues covered below.

Other Issues That Impact Independence

Reactions to the Illegal and Irresponsible Behavior of Some Nonprofit Organizations

The whole sector is weakened when electronic evangelical preachers are found to be squandering contributions on their own excesses, nonprofit organizations are found to participate in the illegal channeling of arms, and when fund raisers are found to skim off most of what is given. Such charlatans who cheat the public in the name of charity are the worst of the worst and deserve the awful publicity they receive, but unfortunately public confidence in the sector as a whole is undermined.

General Questioning of the Effectiveness of Philanthropic and Voluntary Organizations

There seems to be a general perception that philanthropic and voluntary organizations are not well managed. This relates to some of the frauds mentioned above, but it also stems from the lack of effectiveness and responsiveness of many of our own institutions. There is also now a widely held view that such organizations should behave more like businesses. We need to get a better grasp of what constitutes effectiveness and excellence in such organizations. Until and unless we do and begin to apply these lessons more generally, we will continue to face doubts and some cynicism. It's my own impression that the performance of philanthropic and voluntary organizations compares favorably to that of businesses, government bodies, and other human institutions. About one-third are models of excellence, the middle one-third are good to fair, and the bottom one-third are generally ineffective. Going back to my earlier point about the role of the sector, I would observe that operating at or near their best, the good philanthropic and voluntary organizations provide a degree of flexibility that enhances significantly our chances as individuals and as a people to be different and to make a difference. Obviously, we need more of the best.

Skepticism and Cynicism About All Sectors and Institutions

We are in a period when there is decided skepticism, much of it healthy, about most of our institutions, including the church, government, media, foundations, the United Way, big business, and so on. It is to be expected that institutions which perform public functions will receive a great deal of scrutiny. Even when they perform openly and effectively, they will not escape suspicion, and where they are perceived to be secretive, unresponsive, or ineffective, there will be cynicism and scorn.

Current Reexaminations of the Relative Roles of the Three Sectors

Beyond the competition issue, there is an even more significant reexamination of the relative roles of the three sectors—for example, in delivering health services or running colleges. Studies question the validity of exemption for nonprofit hospitals and raise questions about the value of private colleges versus public ones. The place of nonprofit organizations is no longer as distinct as it was in past generations. There is clearly a blurring of the roles of the three sectors, and as a consequence there is a legitimate but jarring and sometimes threatening reexamination of the legitimacy of special tax status for certain types of voluntary organizations as well as for the sector as a whole.

Lack of Public Understanding of the Role of the Sector

Without belaboring points covered earlier, a fundamental problem we face is that the public does not really understand the unique place of philanthropic and voluntary organizations in American society. In turn, policymakers do not grasp what not-for-profit endeavor has meant, means, and should continue to mean to the kind of society we are, or, if they already understand, to realize that all this giving—all this volunteering—all this pluralism and freedom cannot be taken for granted and must be nurtured. To expect philanthropic and voluntary organizations to survive and, more importantly, to thrive in the face of pervasive public policy that discourages and even denigrates voluntary initiative is foolish and ultimately dangerous.

. . . .

There is a blurring of the roles of the three sectors that compounds the already difficult task of interpreting the place of philanthropic and voluntary organizations in our society. The relatively small size of this sector compared with commerce and government leaves it the most vulnerable, particularly to excessive control by government, which sees itself as *the* accountable entity.

One of the immediate consequences of the confusion surrounding who should do what in our society is a reduced emphasis on the independence of philanthropic and voluntary organizations. Between the efforts of voluntary groups to attract government dollars and government's growing efforts to regulate nonprofit activity, the sector's quintessential contribution is being reduced.

There are many roles that nonprofit institutions perform, including providing services and acting as vehicles through which the government fulfills some of its public responsibilities, but their largest contribution to society is the independence they provide for innovation, excellence, criticism, and, where necessary, reform.

My own examinations satisfy me that when the sector is independent and devotes itself to unique functions, it is still relevant and, indeed, is still enormously important. If that is so, it's important to heed the warning of Robert Payton, former director of the Center on Philanthropy at Indiana University: "... the new Britannica overlooks philanthropy ... although its predecessors dealt with it quite adequately. That's the way it goes: one day you take it for granted, and the next day it's gone."

11

The Relationship Between Voluntary Organizations and Government: Constructive Partnerships/ Creative Tensions

As we the people have agreed to address specific responsibilities and functions relating to our organized neighborliness, there have evolved public/private partnerships or public/private competition in most areas of public endeavor.

Given the current mix and trend in public services, the equation has to include the commercial sector, and in the face of growing competition among all three sectors the question

---

Paper presented to the 1986 spring meeting of the National Academy of Public Administration, Washington, D.C.

really becomes, "Who should do the public business and how will it be paid for?"

We are used to parallel services by public, voluntary, and commercial institutions that run hospitals, business colleges, and homes for the aged, but all three sectors have become even more competitive and their roles are becoming even more blurred by the very number and spread of similar services as well as by the common denominator of government funding within them. Whether the field is recreation, cancer research, community theater, alcoholism, preservation, family counselling, job training, urban planning, or cemeteries, all three sectors are involved and the government is providing at least some of the funds through formula grants, categorical grants, block grants, project grants, contracts, loans, loan guarantees, credit insurance, interest subsidies, vouchers, purchase agreements, price supports, surplus land grants, and many other forms of assistance.

Even where it has become obvious that certain activities are the clear responsibility of government, rather than establish facilities or programs the government has very often chosen to fulfill its responsibility through voluntary institutions and, more recently, through business corporations. A relatively recent example relates to health research, now a multi-billion dollar federal enterprise carried forward largely through the universities, with a growing role for private businesses. Today, in almost all areas of public responsibility, including hospitals, schools and colleges, family counseling, maternal and child health, job training for the unemployed, homes for the aged, protection for endangered species, international education, and on and on, this partnership exists.

These partnership arrangements are now being challenged, however, by growing competition among the partners, limited funds, and a concern that the patchwork nature of the system leaves it uncoordinated, unmanageable, and unaccountable.

As with most matters, the dilemma is not altogether new and we can learn something from history. A helpful historical perspective is contributed by Lester Salamon of the Urban Institute, who reminds us of "a classical study of American charities completed by Amos Warner in 1894 which reported that the 200

New York agencies serving orphan children and the friendless were receiving two-thirds of their income from government sources by the [year] 1802, and that half of the expenditures made by New York City for care of the poor went to private charitable organizations."

Salamon adds: "Despite the rhetoric of separation, it is actually cooperation and interdependence that seem to have characterized the relationship between government and the nonprofit sector throughout most of our country's history."

There is and always will be debate about what government's essential responsibilities are, but over the years there has developed a consensus that democratic government has a responsibility to deal with our most basic shared needs—defense, sewage disposal, clean water, communicable disease, public education, social security, and many other manifestations of our abject interdependence.

Voluntary organizations, unlike government, are not usually established to deal with "the general welfare." They tend to deal with *Lutheran* aged, the school in *my* neighborhood, *autistic* children, or *modern* art. They represent alternatives, options, experimentation, supplementation, and leadership, and they can be a vehicle through which government fulfills many of its public functions. It is essential to our clear grasp of their relative roles, however, that for basic governmental responsibility it is our representative democratic government to which we turn.

This doesn't mean that government must run every service and program, but that's a secondary consideration. We won't clearly sort out the primary issue unless we start with an understanding of ultimate responsibility. Whatever delivery mechanisms we may want to establish for these governmental services, they are, in the final analysis, a governmental responsibility. We can say we want the churches to play a larger role in delivering essential social services or that we want voluntary organizations to carry a larger share of services for the elderly, but we can no longer allow our delivery preferences to obscure the fact that these are government responsibilities. Though the activity can be delegated, the responsibility cannot.

It is of course necessary to address financial responsibility. Here, too, though the issue is enormously complicated, the underlying principle is simple. But because it's so tough to swallow, we prefer to start almost anywhere else. Over the years, I have tried to avoid the basic conclusion that if it is government's responsibility, then government financing should underpin the effort. I'm a great believer in contributions, fees for service, vouchers, and other means by which the values of the marketplace are applied to making services available and keeping them effective, responsive, and economical, but whatever funding patterns are appropriate and possible, making certain that governmental services are in fact funded is ultimately government's responsibility.

The city or county may have an ambulance service of its own, contract with a profit or nonprofit organization to provide ambulance service, or allow competition among all three, but it has the ultimate responsibility to be certain that the service is available, accessible, and affordable to all.

Having placed so bluntly before you the limitations of voluntary organizations to be responsible for the general welfare, let me also deal with the limitations of big government to carry out the staggering responsibilities I place so squarely on it.

The primary limitations relate to the size and diversity of our nation. We want services and systems that are manageable, coordinated, and accountable, and this leads us constantly towards centralization, which in this country gets things totally out of scale. Even at the state level, Columbus or Sacramento are just too far from the people to be able to deliver most public services. I recall the experiment in California where, for purposes of coordination and management, responsibility for most human services was centralized in one mammoth department. The system was designed to make certain that people did not fall through the cracks between health, welfare, housing, rehabilitation, and the other human services. The problem was that the cracks became chasms. The department was so large and was so far removed from Eureka or San Diego that it soon became grossly expensive and totally inefficient. Its size and remoteness made it completely insensitive to the people it was designed to serve and inaccessible to their elected representatives as well.

Another practical problem was that it could not attract talented people, such as health department directors from other states, because they did not want to be three or four layers down in such an omnibus department.

In the past fifty years, we have expanded enormously what is considered governmental responsibility. As the scope of these responsibilities has grown, we have turned more and more to the federal government for financing and other leadership. The national character of many of these problems, the limitations imposed by the tax base of state and local governments, and the limitations of funds voluntarily contributed have all caused us to look to Washington.

Even though we may be emotionally and intellectually commited to dispersion of authority, that commitment is challenged by day-to-day realities and our own conflicting desires.

We don't want one monolithic federal system for health care or social services, for example, but we do stridently insist that the systems that do exist are coordinated, comprehensive, and accountable.

We don't want more federal government—*except* in the areas which *we* view as a priority. If our priority is the criminal justice system, or cancer control, or clean air, or the rights of minorities or women, or learning disabilities, we can be exceedingly articulate and forceful in making the case that the federal government, as the representative of all the people, has a moral responsibility to deal with that priority. And the listing is not limited to human suffering—witness the recent clamor about federal cuts in the National Endowment for the Arts.

Our solution has been to point up federal responsibility and to evolve a decentralized delivery system involving partnerships among the levels of government and between government and the other two sectors.

This pattern of financing and delivering public services has now reached a point of such complexity that many people consider it unresponsive, ineffective, incapable of accountability, and utterly beyond management.

We have tended to deal with the dilemma of decentralization vis-à-vis coordination of services by building complex systems involving a mix of governmental levels and non-governmental institutions and then damn the system because it is not accountable or manageable.

And faced with repeated breakdowns of these complex systems, Congress, which talks so much about community control, tightens its control and, as a result, the federal government overlays stifling control mechanisms to try to be sure that everyone is playing the role that the federal government believes is appropriate for them. The result is a profusion of pluralism fighting against centralization of funding, centralization of planning, and centralization of authority.

Into this muddle have come extremists who say:

1. Voluntary organizations did it before and should do it again; or
2. If you want it done right, turn it over to those with bottom-line discipline, the business sector; or
3. If it's government's business, government should do it.

Many public administrators, legislators, and others are now insisting that we must move to a much more clearly delineated governmental system that is *not* confused by contractual arrangements and other delegations of governmental responsibility.

As we try to sort this all out, it's essential to keep in mind the kind of people with whom I worked for so many years, the discharged mental hospital patients dumped by state hospital systems into unprepared community systems, now newly discovered as among the tragic homeless. They have the total range of needs—physical health, mental health, food, employment, housing—but these confused souls are usually dropped into a community system without anyone being responsible for helping them through the maze of federal, state, and local programs, not to mention voluntary and proprietary services. It helps to think of these tortured human beings when sorting out responsibility and effective delivery systems.

It starts with governmental responsibility.

We need to make a distinction between government's responsibility, the mechanisms for delivering government services, and how we keep services accountable and responsive.

A fundamental decision will relate to whether we go for a streamlined, easily identifiable, top-down governmental structure or continue to try to do our government's business through the more complex mix of governmental levels, voluntary institutions, and proprietary organizations.

There are attractions to a more clearly delineated governmental system, but people of all political and philosophical persuasions have concluded that trying to do much of this country's business from Washington, or Harrisburg, or Albany just doesn't work.

On the other hand, one can get carried away with the rhetoric of pluralism, dispersion of authority, and decentralization and overlook the clear evidence of breakdown in such essential factors as coordination and accountability.

After years of struggling with the dilemma in some very tangible settings, I have come to favor a system that starts with governmental responsibility but provides for many different avenues by which that responsibility can be fulfilled.

I recall a conversation with one of the most senior and able people in the field of human services. Margaret Hickey, public affairs editor of *Ladies Home Journal*, chairwoman of President Truman's Commission on Women, and now well into her seventies, still has a remarkably fresh way of looking at things, and this, combined with her depth and breadth of experience, makes her a sage counselor. We were talking about how to organize human services, and, drawing on her years of witnessing the pendulum swing back and forth between centralization and decentralization and of seeing various bright ideas being pasted by the federal government on unwitting states and communities, she concluded that in this continent-wide nation, comprising such diversity, we just can't expect any one model to be right, or that the federal government will ever develop the omniscience to figure out what's best for the citizens of Roaring Fork, Los Angeles, and Bangor. She concluded that the best we can do is to stipulate the basic services that should be provided along with the basic attributes that should be present and then let local people do it their way. I realize that sounds rather simplistic, but I sure have learned to lean in that direction rather than the opposite.

I get discouraged when we repeatedly assume that there is any one solution to solving the complexity of human need. For what it's worth, my experience is that there is no simple approach, but that there is a formula which involves:

1. availability of service;

2. accessibility of service;
3. affordability;
4. coordination; and
5. consumer influence on the services designed to serve them.

The questions of availability, accessibility, and affordability come smack up against the realities of resources, but I think the American people want and will pay for good services. I believe that much of the taxpayer revolt involves a rebellion against having to pay for poor, insensitive, and overpriced services.

As people are finding out that cutbacks mean grandmother doesn't get housekeeping services, or neighbors don't get enough food, or crippled kids don't get special education services, or working women don't have day care, the reaction is "My God, we didn't mean that!" Local and state governments, usually far more strapped than the federal government, are digging deeper to keep or restore such services, but are also organizing them so that they are more effective, sensitive, and economical.

As a society, we can afford, and I believe will be willing to pay for, *good* public services, but the lesson must be utterly clear that the public will not tolerate systems that are not effective or fair, including services that are run for the convenience of the providers and not the consumers.

I don't mean to suggest that the sky is the limit on spending, but I believe that we want, need, and will pay for effective government services. I also believe that as the responsibility for planning, organizing, and evaluating those services is more broadly shared, we will be better prepared to make some excruciatingly difficult decisions that involve saying no, even in the face of awful human consequences. We will decide not to keep the dying alive at any cost and we will also decide that we have to set realistic limits on the price the government will pay for dialysis or heart surgery or psychoanalysis. The leaders coming up through the ranks are "street smart"—they can tolerate *and* encourage the democratic cacophony, but after listening to the strains of joy and pain, they will be able to say no—sometimes even to you and me.

The most serious missing elements in my formula are not money or talent or will, but the elements of consumer influence and administrative coordination for such a decentralized pluralistic system.

If, after years as a community organizer, I had to emphasize any one factor that is most likely to provide responsive, sensitive, effective service, it would be the element of consumer influence, including and, indeed, emphasizing consumer involvement in articulating needs, planning services, operating programs, and evaluating results. The more I work with communities, the more faith I develop in the common sense of people and their capacity to respond to responsibility with fairness and practicality.

For many people and services, the market theory and approach will be the most direct way to achieve consumer influence. This deserves far more positive attention than space permits, but because it has received a good deal of deserved coverage elsewhere, let me comment on some of its limitations, at least in terms of what purchasing power *can't* do.

In certain communities and for many major programs, it may never be practical to give people a choice for their hospital, school, museum, or senior center. The Minnesota Citizens League says that one way to overcome practical limitations on day-to-day competition is to give elected and appointed officials more options as to whether they contract with for-profit or not-for-profit groups to handle ambulance services or garbage removal. Contracts would be subject to periodic renewal and appointed and elected officials would be free to switch from one approach to another. I would go a step further and provide regular voter referenda on the responsiveness and effectiveness of major services; when approval falls below certain levels, the service provider would be given a year or two to improve its operations before facing the voters again.

Another means of ensuring consumer and citizen involvement, but one we've never gotten very good at, involves citizen boards and advisory committees for schools, health services, urban transportation, corrections, and even military research planning. We in public administration and the other fields of public service are just not very good at working with such groups; in fact, we're pretty terrible. We tend to equate success with masterful manipulation, and we certainly don't train or even condition our people for the realities and opportunities created by an active citizenry.

Elected officials are, of course, one of the best ways to keep government responsive to the people. But even here we need more attention to such basics as voter registration, voter turnout, regional governance, and the training of elected officials in all sorts of responsibilities, including the balance between prodding the system and supporting it.

Whatever the devices for encouraging rather than discouraging or neglecting citizen participation, the goal should be to give people maximum influence over the programs designed to serve them.

The second neglected element in making decentralized systems work, the effective administration of such pluralistic arrangements, will also require commitment to individuals, particularly those who are most vulnerable or have multiple needs. Without being entirely sure of my ground, let me go out on a limb and suggest that the group that moves into this disparate system and fits the pieces together *for* the consumer will eventually become the de facto manager of the system and, thus, among the most important of our public servants. For example, there is a desperate need for more manager/coordinators within state and county human-service departments, and there is a like need for client/managers for people with multiple needs.

One of the very best programs I ever saw involved volunteers called "community friends" who were carefully trained in the complexities of state/local human care systems and who were assigned to persons discharged from state mental hospitals or just entering community mental health systems. It was the responsibility of each "community friend" to stay with that individual until he or she was connected with and attended by all necessary services. The program was under the direction of a social worker who knew the pain of these human beings, knew the system, respected the capacity of volunteers, and knew how to use both people and experience as leverage to improve the system.

That role is in the best tradition of social workers, who are supposed to be oriented to individuals and families (and not limited to health or psychology), knowledgeable about the system, and involved with all its parts, including schools, courts, job agencies, food banks, alcoholism treatment centers, hospitals, self-help groups, and so on. If they could just expand on that orientation and experience and match it with the need for making even broader systems work for people, then the even more golden days of social work could still lie ahead.

There is, of course, a practical limitation on professions and professionals to be oriented to the whole person, and there has been a natural tendency for professions and professionals to become focused on credentials, licensing, and practice. The system of the future, however, will depend on maximum citizen participation. Social work is the profession that pioneered community organization, but along with other professions it let a commendable concern for professional standards freeze out the non-professional and the consumer in shaping human services.

Whether the expanded role of representing the consumer in the dispersed system is provided by a new order of case work, a reconstituted family agency, a new volunteer corps, a sub-specialty of public administration, or a combination of these isn't clear. What is clear is that if we are committed to a decentralized system of government services, someone has to be responsible for the consumers who are not in a position to exercise their options and who, in a humane, democratic society, have a right to be served, represented, and empowered.

There is one other important relationship between nonprofit organizations and government in the provision of services. Understandably, we tend to focus on the direct delivery of services and to not speak much of the role of voluntary organizations in creating, shaping, and changing government services. There is certainly about as much confusion and competition as most of us can handle in just trying to build and blend the dispersed delivery mechanisms, without getting into the advocacy role of not-for-profit organizations. However, if we really want to understand and shape the broader context of how government services are decided and provided, we have to develop a higher tolerance for "creative tension."

Advocacy is easily tolerated by public officials who start the groundswell in the first place, or who at least encourage enthusiastic supporters. If you've ever worked with (or perhaps it's more accurately stated as worked for!) such outreachers as Jim

Shannon, Bob Felix, Burt Brown, or Jim Webb, you have known some of the absolute masters at marshalling organized citizen demand for more of what they just happen to want. Presidents might argue to keep a lid on mental-health expenditures, but baby-faced Bob Felix would innocently say he couldn't help it if all those people from Alabama and Rhode Island were telling Senator Hill and Representative Fogarty that mental-health appropriations should be doubled.

. . . .

We say that we are all for pluralism and active citizenship in the abstract, but we are not very sophisticated in dealing with them day-to-day in our own work. There was an apt observation in the chapter entitled "The Role of Philanthropy in a Changing Society," from the Peterson Commission Report of the '60s: "There are some who may agree 'in principle' with the worth of private philanthropy but, when a crunch is on, they view philanthropy as Lord Melbourne, Prime Minister of England in the early years of Queen Victoria's reign, viewed religion. 'I have,' said he, 'as much respect for religion as the next person. But things have come to a pretty pass when religion is allowed to interfere with England's interest.'"

There are many roles that voluntary organizations play, including providing services and acting as vehicles through which the government fulfills some of its public responsibilities, but their largest contribution is the independence they provide for innovation, advocacy, criticism, and, where necessary, reform.

In the pursuit of government's responsibilities to operate and improve services and keep them responsive to the people, we must develop public administrators who are conditioned to and comfortable with the pluralism that governs how this country decides and conducts its public business.

David Mathews helps pull it all together when he says that the best way to understand how this country really operates is to think of it as "Coalition America."

Our democracy—our liberty—our freedom—still depend on informed citizen participation, and we presage the decline of our civilization if we think the issues utterly beyond citizen comprehension. We can be discouraged by the complexity of today's issues and concerned that people won't make the right decisions for themselves, their families, and their communities, but there is wisdom and comfort still in Thomas Jefferson's advice: "I know of no safe depository of the ultimate powers of society, but the people themselves; and if we think them not enlightened enough to exercise their control with a wholesome discretion, the remedy is not to take it from them, but to inform their discretion by education."

Chester Newland, Donald Stone, Harlan Cleveland, Guthrie Birkhead, George Frederickson, Frederick Mosher, and others have provided recent reminders that the origins of the field of public administration were tied closely to the involvement of public-spirited citizens in achieving good government. This is supported in recent re-readings of some basic texts, including Luther Gulick's reminiscences about the National Institute and the National Bureau.

I suggest that public administration, like other disciplines and professions, has gotten altogether too far from the citizen and that active citizenship is at the heart of providing good services, protecting rights, and fulfilling the many other responsibilities of democratic government.

I commend the Academy for this effort to better understand how public services can be best provided and I commend the National Association of Schools of Public Administration for their similar interests, and I respectfully suggest that both expand their attention to the encouragement of active citizenship and to the development of public administrators who have a clear grasp of how the public business is done and who also have a capacity for what my professor and dean, Paul Appleby, said was our task—". . . to make a mesh of things."

12
Community Foundations: More of the Best

MY PREPARATION FOR THIS assignment has been in two parts. From my experience as a community organizer and with some knowledge of what is happening in and to the independent sector as a whole, I've tried to develop an image of the ideal performance of the community foundation of the future. Simultaneously, I've tried to learn more about the community foundation of the present.

As with most invited papers, I approached the task with puffery and fantasy. I expected to find a wide disparity between what should be and what is, and that I would thus be credited with leading you along the right path.

Alas for me, but hurrah for you, the two parts of my study converged in the many magnificent examples already at hand of the community foundation at its best. I repeatedly found myself

---

An invited paper for the Council of Community Foundations conference, "The Community Foundation: A New Perception," October 1981, Monterey, California.

"discovering" a new right way, but no sooner would I dash for the rainbow than I would find some of you already there. I quickly concluded that a change for the better is, as usual, just more of the best.

The Role of Foundations From the Broader Perspective of Our National Values and the Nation's Fundamental Institutions

The values are:

> Freedom
> Worth and dignity of the individual
> Opportunity
> Justice
> Mutual responsibility

The fundamental vehicles through which this nation attempts to preserve and enhance its basic values are:

Representative government starting with one person/one vote
The freedoms of speech and assembly
A free press
A system of justice based on due process and presumption of innocence
Universal public education
Free enterprise

Beyond the formal structures that exist to maintain the basic values of a free society, there are less formal networks that serve those ends and also provide outlets for individual expression and growth. These include:

Family
Religion
Community
Neighborhood
Voluntary associations

The role of foundations is to help make the formal and informal systems work in the service of the larger values.

You are that *unimportant* in the hierarchy of necessity. But you are that *important* in your capacity to enhance the effectiveness of our more fundamental institutions.

It is important to your orientation to realize that those fundamental institutions can function without you, but it is also important to your orientation *and* your morale to know that they function ever so much better when you are at your best.

It is also helpful to get the proportions in perspective. The federal budget is $800 billion. State and local governments add another $500 billion. Funds spent by voluntary organizations total $150 billion. Of this, $50 billion comes from contributions. (Approximately one-third comes from government and one-third from user fees such as tuition.) Foundations represent $2.5 billion in annual allocations, or 5 percent of all giving. Community foundations represent $100 million in annual allocations. This represents 4 percent of foundation giving and one-fifth of 1 percent of all voluntary giving.

A look at the community also helps to provide perspective. Responsibilities are shifting to it at a time when its financial base is at its weakest. Paul Ylvisaker's "The Urban Issues" provides these examples:

Movement of jobs and people
Growing urban underclass
Decaying infrastructure
Devolving governmental arrangements
Shortage of housing

As part of an overview it is useful to catalog your assets:

Board members and other participants
The opportunity for review
An aura of influence
Some degree of objectivity and neutrality
Influence with donors
Continuity
Money

In the composite, these assets add up to real power far beyond the dollars involved.

I end this overview with what I think are some reasonable deductions:

1. Government is overwhelmingly the major source of public expenditure and service.
2. The $100 million represented by community foundations is so small as to be inconsequential measured against the budgets and problems of our communities.
3. The total influence of community foundations can be significant to the extent it empowers and multiplies larger forces—namely, the fundamental institutions and processes that preserve and enhance our basic values, as well as the less formal networks that also serve those ends while providing outlets for individual expression and growth.

Implications for Program Focus

There are obviously many ideas and suggestions that grow out of any such analysis, but in the interest of time and particularly of emphasis, let me hold to three:

1. Greater Emphasis on Making Government More Effective

During the past year, I've been spending a good deal of time at meetings of foundation representatives where, as at this session, the topic generally relates to the changing or future role of foundations. In most of these sessions, I have attempted to lay out a view of the major needs of the times, including such urgent issues as governance of our cities, population control, structural unemployment, nuclear proliferation, international understanding, eradication of cancer, strengthening public education, and conservation of water and land.

I've been told repeatedly that each of these is utterly beyond the capacity of the foundations at hand, and that indeed almost all are so large in scope and cost that they have to be left to government. It has also been my general observation that most of these foundation leaders prefer to be somewhat aloof from, and are inclined to be critical of, government. They have quickly brought the discussion back to the basic question: "What can *we* do that is unique and important?" My answer in all such cases has been: "Use your power and influence to make *our* government more effective, including its capacity to deal with the big issues."

To me, this is the primary role of voluntary institutions. Democratic government is the fundamental representative of the people when problems and aspirations require the ultimate expression of organized neighborliness. Therefore, making government work is far more important than all the other worthwhile things we do. It is certainly clear in my mind that it is the primary function of *community* foundations.

You know your field far better than I, but for what it's worth here are some areas where your assets, including leverage, can make an important difference:

a. the structure of government, including the basic design of city council and the organization of departments and bureaus;
b. the funding base for municipal operating expenses, including regional arrangements and responsibilities;
c. the process of governance, such as:

1) voter registration and turnout
2) the electoral system
3) open government
4) the relative roles and powers of the mayor, the council, and the school board;
5) the relative roles of city, county, and state; and
6) citizen involvement and impact

d. long-range planning;
e. special studies, such as:
1) public education;
2) the municipal court system;
3) transportation;
4) the balance between centralization and decentralization; and
5) alternative service delivery systems.
f. stimulation of effective public/private partnerships;
g. development and encouragement of citizen organizations, which might be the regular advocates and watchdogs for neighborhoods, police protection, open government, good schools, equal opportunity, and so on. The foundation should not attempt to be the community council for better government or the citizen's committee for better schools, but it should encourage such groups, particularly when it comes to strengthening their capacity for regular oversight.

2. Greater Emphasis on Strengthening Private Philanthropy in the Community

The emphasis should be on expanding and strengthening giving per se (i.e., to the causes of one's choice). Here are some examples of "more of the best."

a. stimulation and assistance for corporate philanthropy;

b. encouragement and assistance to well-to-do persons;
c. providing leadership for banks and lawyers in effective and responsive philanthropy;
d. providing leadership for other foundations in the region, particularly as it relates to their understanding of their stake in the success of the community;
e. providing leadership for national foundations, particularly as it relates to their understanding of community and current priorities;
f. emphasizing grants that are specifically designed to build the independent fund-raising capacity of the voluntary organizations supported; and
g. employment of a fundraiser or use of fund-raising consultants to work with recipient organizations to help build their independent income.

3. A Suggestion for a New Activity to Strengthen the Community's Independent Sector as a Whole: Establishment of at Least One Center in Every Significant Metropolitan Area That Would:

a. provide graduate training and degrees in management of philanthropic and voluntary organizations;
b. represent visible evidence for young people that this is a major career area;
c. provide training and continuing education for persons with responsibilities for corporate philanthropy, foundation activity, and voluntary organizations;
d. provide training for board members;
e. develop a research capacity for studies in and on the sector;
f. encourage academic departments and disciplines to see this sector as a legitimate and attractive area for education and research;

g. serve as a meeting ground for researchers and practitioners;
h. be a haven for practitioners to reflect and write during special breaks awarded by their boards and by the center;
i. produce regular publications; and
j. provide a neutral space for the study and possible resolution of problems within the sector.

This sector is a major employer (10 percent of the U.S. workforce is employed in the sector), but there are relatively few training programs for persons with responsibility for philanthropic and voluntary organizations. It is increasingly obvious that we have to make these institutions even more effective. There is a central role and opportunity for any community foundation in helping generate interest and support for such a center in its community.

Can You Change, Even if You Want To?

Take stock from John Gardner's book, *Self-Renewal: The Individual and the Innovative Society*.

> Some of our most difficult problems today are such as to defy correction by any single dramatic solution. They will yield, if at all, only to a whole series of innovations. An example may be found in the renewal of our metropolitan areas. To bring these sprawling giants back under the rational control of the people who live in them will require a prolonged burst of political, economic and social innovation.
> The renewal of societies and organizations can go forward only if someone cares. Apathy and lowered motivation are the most widely noted characteristics of a civilization in decline. Apathetic men and women accomplish nothing. Those who believe in nothing change nothing for the better. They renew nothing and heal no one, least of all themselves. Anyone who understands our situation at all knows that we are in little danger of failing through lack of

material strength. If we falter, it will be a failure of heart and spirit.

Imagine that you're finally seventy-five years old and looking back. How will you hope that you dealt with this responsibility?

The current financial crunch facing our communities, with its frightening mix of increased expectations and decreased funding, should be seized as the rationale, motivation, and opportunity to force change. You have a unique opportunity and obligation. You're not indispensable, but you can make a very large difference. These can be *very* great years for the aggressive and effective community foundation.

I envy the role and the opportunity and even some of the challenging problems which, for what it's worth, don't seem, at least at this distance, to be overwhelming. More importantly, the task itself seems doable.

It comes down to "more of the best."

The Strategic Links Between Business and the Nonprofit Sector

IN 1989, I SERVED as chairman of a Salzburg Seminar that attempted to ascertain the state of pluralism in various countries and cultures. For two weeks and through advance study of resource material, fifty participants compared views and experiences about private initiative in their very different countries. Though our focus was on voluntary initiative as expressed by private philanthropy and community service, it was obvious that the larger interest was pluralistic opportunities of every form, including free enterprise. Intense interest in and encouraging signs of multiple outlets for creativity and influence were evident

---

Excerpts from Chapter 3, "The Strategic Links Between Business and the Nonprofit Sector," by Brian O'Connell, from *The Corporate Contributions Handbook*, edited by James P. Shannon. San Francisco: Jossey-Bass Publishers (in cooperation with the Council on Foundations), 1991.

in the nations of Eastern Europe, such as Hungary and Poland; underdeveloped countries, such as Uganda and India; and the developed countries, such as Germany and Japan.

The very notion of pluralism, upon which the voluntary sector rests, can be seen in the variety of forms of free expression we now see emerging in many countries. Factors encouraging free expression vary by country and culture but include:

- pressure from the people for change, power, and improved services;
- pressure from within the government to tap the self-interest, time, talent, and money of the people to develop or maintain services;
- pressure from outside bodies such as the World Bank, foundations, corporations, international private voluntary organizations (PVOs), and religious groups to accelerate development; and a
- growing awareness by people and governments of the practical limitations of big government, whatever its form or ideology.

When people from Senegal or Thailand discuss opportunities for creativity and influence, they are equally interested in commercial and voluntary endeavors, and they recognize that the common denominator of both is the freedom of individuals to pursue their own ideas. The same freedom that allows a would-be entrepreneur to incorporate a new for-profit business allows any other citizen to form a nonprofit corporation. In the American system of private enterprise, for-profit and nonprofit groups are partners in their mutual and freely pursued efforts to determine the needs of a dynamic society and to find creative and efficient ways of meeting these needs.

The specialness of the American commercial and voluntary sectors is often recognized more clearly by people from other countries. If we accept that our patterns and levels of participation and generosity make important contributions to our national life, it then becomes important for us to understand and nurture the roots that give rise to such pluralism.

Many perceptive American businesspeople undertand that our voluntary and commercial opportunities are inescapably linked under the banner of private enterprise and are mutually dependent on our rights to freely engage in such private initiatives. Randall Meyers, former president of Exxon, USA, says that what is at stake in both voluntary and commercial opportunities is "freedom, whether it is expressed in the freedom to state one's beliefs, to teach different philosophies, to form social or labor organizations, or to pursue a business opportunity." He goes on to say "that all private institutions are harmed when the ability of any one to pursue its legitimate role in society is impaired" (Meyers, 1979).

In an article entitled "We Must Help Each Other," Elvis Stahr, who has had the benefit of viewing the American scene from many different perspectives—Audubon Society president, corporate director, secretary of the army, university president—says that the profit and nonprofit spheres "must help each other if we expect to attain the independence and freedom that mean so much to us all" (Stahr, 1979).

John D. Rockefeller 3rd, in the article "America's Threatened Third Sector," says it is essential that all three sectors of our society remain strong. "As long as each sector is healthy, we will preserve our uniqueness, our diversity, the source of much of our strength and creativity—and our best hope for a promising future." He continues, "Two of the sectors are recognizable to everyone: business and government. But the third, the private nonprofit sector, is so little understood that I am tempted to call it 'the invisible sector'" (Rockefeller, 1978).

. . . .

If voluntary organizations are an integral part of private enterprise, why are they not more like business? In my thirty-five years with voluntary organizations, one of the greatest challenges has been to capitalize on the interest and ability of corporate executives without letting the many different characteristics of voluntary organizations get in the way of the enthusiasm and effectiveness of those executives. The greatest frustration for businesspeople working with nonprofits is the difficulty inherent in defining and measuring the success of nonprofit enterprises.

Voluntary organizations do not simply measure success by the bottom line. Many businesspeople who serve with voluntary groups want desperately for the organizations to mirror what they know best, and they are extremely impatient with their nonprofit counterparts. They may assume and claim that voluntary organizations generally are inefficient and poorly managed. I have routinely heard businesspeople make observations such as "These do-gooders just don't know how to manage" or "If we could just get more management discipline into these cause-oriented organizations, they would be far more effective."

My own observation is that these perceptions are often inaccurate and unfair. Voluntary organizations, like businesses and other human institutions, vary in their effectiveness. About one-third of businesses and voluntary organizations are models of excellence, one-third are good to fair, and the other third are poorly managed and generally ineffective. To determine whether a nonprofit organization is effective, it is important for businesspeople to have a clear understanding of what is unique about these organizations, both in the social role they fulfill as well as in the ways they operate. If we simply apply bottom-line efficiency as the standard, we run the risk of ignoring the special characteristics of dynamic voluntary organizations.

Many attempts to identify the unique profile of nonprofits tend toward quantification, such as determining the number of board meetings held, the dollars raised, or the number of clients served, and omit any analysis of such factors as social impact or influence on quality of life that are often the true measure of the effectiveness of these groups.

I have worked on evaluation teams with business leaders looking at voluntary organizations and have often been surprised that my corporate counterparts will present a very negative appraisal compared to mine. They might even say that the organization is the epitome of poor management and point out its failure to have adequate bylaws, minutes, a planning process, or an annual report. On the other hand, I will give high marks to the same break-all-the-rules group because I see evidence of real influence on the community trying to improving its schools, mass transit, or other public services, or trying to provide humane services to vulnerable populations that no one else has discovered, such as elderly patients who would stay in their homes if someone would just provide repairs. A great many voluntary organizations are both dynamic and efficient, and all should strive for both. But if I have to settle for one characteristic, it will be dynamism.

Cecily Cannan Selby (1978), former national director of the Girl Scouts, called for nonprofit organizations to be more effective but not always with the business model in mind: "In using the term nonprofit, which refers to a financial balance sheet only, perhaps we obscure the essence of this sector of our society, which is indeed to be profitable to citizens, business and government—to benefit its constituents, its clients and its employees. This sector has found, and one hopes will continue to find, new and better ways to preserve and enhance pluralism, voluntarism, and the distinctiveness of art, intellect and charity."

Businesspeople may be impressed by the results nonprofit organizations achieve measured against costs. In Peter Drucker's recent article, "What Business Can Learn from Nonprofits" (1989), he underscores how much voluntary groups accomplish with the combination of maximum caring and minimum cost. He admires their effective utilization of volunteers and boards and their ability to stretch a dollar so much further than business. He says, for example: "As a rule, nonprofits are more money-conscious than business enterprises are. They talk and worry about money much of the time because it is so hard to raise and because they always have so much less of it than they need."

Recently, I was comparing business and voluntary organizations with Andrew Heiskell, former CEO of Time Inc., who has probably had as much exposure to both types of organization as anyone. In a personal conversation with me, Heiskell said that he had come to believe that "voluntary organizations demand much more of themselves than most businesses, and they get much more out of their boards, staff, and dollars."

Even in large nonprofit organizations, businesspeople tend to overlook factors that help make these groups effective. When I was national director of the Mental Health Association, new board members with corporate backgrounds would invariably state that the board of fifty-one was too large, that there were too few administrative staff members, or that, for efficiency, we should consider merging with the Retardation Association. They did not understand the need to involve as many people as was feasible and to keep citizens mobilized around causes they care passionately about.

Businesspeople know little about keeping volunteers involved, enthusiastic, and effective. Volunteers are unpaid and therefore even more independent than employees, and there are far more volunteers per staff supervisor than employees. Voluntary groups are quite different from businesses because of their need to constantly achieve maximum community involvement, the demands of fundraising, the dearth of advertising budgets, and far lower salaries. In the March/April 1989 issue of *Across the Board*, published by the Conference Board, several former business executives indicated that they thought their transfer to full-time roles on the voluntary side would be "a piece of cake," but all of them had retreated to the corporate ranks as a result of the dizzying complexity of working with artists, faculty, independent-minded boards, fund-raising groups, and staff and resources totally inadequate to meet obligations. Voluntary organizations can learn a great deal from business about good management, staff development, planning, evaluation of results, and much more, but these are often not the primary ingredients contributing to their effectiveness and the fulfillment of their unique role in American society.

Although there are very real differences between for-profit and nonprofit organizations, both types of organizations are nevertheless parts of America's distinctive private enterprise system. In concluding his piece on the third sector, Rockefeller says, "If voluntary giving lags, we will be well on our way toward a two-sector system. Opportunities and incentives for individual initiative will disappear, and the vaunted pluralism of American society will gradually give way to a monolithic system."

Both the for-profit and nonprofit sides of private enterprise are faced with growing domination by government. The nonprofit side seems to be the weaker in dealing with what Senator Daniel Patrick Moynihan (1980) calls "the growing monopoly of government." He and many others point out that if this so-called third sector becomes further dominated by government, we will in fact have only two sectors and, inevitably, just one sector. In the long run, the vitality of all private initiative depends upon its truly being free enterprise.

14

Corporate Philanthropy: Getting Bigger, Broader, and Tougher to Manage

FOR TEN YEARS, corporate giving has been the fastest growing side of U.S. philanthropy. In each of the four years from 1982 to 1985, it grew more than 10 percent, and over the decade 1975–1985 it grew by some 250 percent. The annual dollar giving of corporations now ranks close to the total from all private foundations. Each contributes approximately $4 billion. When non-cash allocations such as donated goods and services are counted in, corporate philanthropy is larger by far.

Corporate public service is also more diverse and complicated than foundation grantmaking, involving as it does the breadth of matching gifts, decentralized grantmaking at plant

---

Keynote address at the National Conference on Corporate Philanthropy sponsored by the Public Affairs Council, 1987, and reprinted in *Corporate Philanthropy*, INDEPENDENT SECTOR, August/September 1987.

locations, loaned executives, the encouragement of volunteering, leadership roles in many community organizations, donations of goods and services, and much, much more.

When IBM won the first Harvard Business School/Dively Award for Corporate Public Initiative in 1985, the corporation was cited for its vast array of public services, including job training for nonprofits, social service leaves, a computer literacy program, training programs for school administrators, an extensive matching gifts program, one of the highest annual grant-making totals, and so on.

Corporate philanthropy is getting bigger, broader, and much tougher to manage.

The scope of corporate public service has grown so fast that many companies are just now realizing that they have to plan as carefully for it as for their other responsibilities. For other corporations, the size, visibility, and assumed responsibilities of public service are now of such proportions that, for both external and internal reasons, they impose themselves on the organization's strategic planning and priority operations.

One of the best descriptions of how a corporation should target its charitable activity concluded with the apt phrase that a company's public service should be "at the crossroads where company and public interests intersect." In 1978, the Weyerhaeuser organization conducted what is still one of the most comprehensive studies of a company's public-service program. Prompted by concerns that the corporation had been donating money to projects too far removed from the company's identifiable interest and strengths, the review gave Weyerhaeuser the opportunity to study the rationale and priorities for its future program. After considering all the advice about being public serving or self-serving, the company concluded that it should focus its giving "at the crossroads where company and public interests intersect." Within that definition, the company decided to give considerable attention to the preservation of forests, a topic it knows a great deal about and has a stake in.

There are other good examples of companies trying to be "at the crossroads." In the September 21, 1981, issue of *Fortune*, Lee Smith wrote that because Interspace deals with clay, steel, and aluminum, it was natural for the company to contribute to the development and display of sculpture. He also reported that in the mid-1970s, General Motors, seeking to improve its management/recruiting program, decided to concentrate most of its generous education grants on thirteen business schools and fourteen engineering schools it deemed crucial to its own future. In an October 1980 *Nation's Business* piece, Kenneth L. Albrecht, then vice president at Equitable, is quoted as saying: "There is really no point in any corporation wasting its time on matters in which it has no interest and with which it is not equipped to deal. For example, Equitable—as a life, health and pension company—will almost always have a segment of its program devoted to health. If we made musical instruments, our interest in the performing arts would likely be great."

One of the pitfalls many companies fell into and still struggle with involves the natural tendency to model themselves after private foundations. It was natural that as companies became philanthropic, they tended to follow the older and distinguished pattern represented by well-established foundations. Many companies still try to emulate their counterparts in the foundation world. They do the same things—they even organize themselves the same ways—and so they lose the chance to capitalize on their uniqueness. More recently, corporate leaders have begun to understand how different corporate philanthropy can and should be. To a much greater extent than private foundations, corporations have a range of opportunities to influence change. Indeed, those opportunities are exactly why John Kenneth Galbraith believes that corporations should not be allowed to make contributions—he says it gives them the chance to exercise undue influence. The best company programs are those that encourage employee giving and volunteering, involve the company in public/private partnerships, provide program-related investments, and in every other way use their dollars and other assets to effect change.

. . . .

The matching-gift program was started by General Electric in 1955, matching approximately $200,000 in employee contributions to colleges. By 1980, more than 900 companies were participating in the education "match," producing almost $40 million for higher education that year. The total in matching funds donated to these and other nonprofit organizations was more than $100 million.

According to Lee Smith, General Electric started the matching-gifts program "as a fringe benefit meant to attract and retain employees." Andrew Heiskell, a former Time Inc. CEO, described the matching-gifts program to me as one of the best means of boosting employee morale and building goodwill for an organization that supports the causes chosen by its employees. Heiskell argues that about 50 percent of a corporation's giving should be "employee driven." Others argue that a company should target a larger proportion for special projects where large sums can make a real difference. Whatever the proportion, GE started something that has influenced philanthropy profoundly.

Honeywell was a 1983 winner of the President's Voluntary Action Award for its support and encouragement of volunteering by employees and retirees. Among the strategies Honeywell uses to increase involvement as volunteers are:

- Community Service Awards—Once-in-a-lifetime grants of $500 to organizations in which employees are active volunteers.
- Management Assistance Project (MAP)—Volunteers provide technical and management assistance to area nonprofit organizations.
- HELP (Honeywell Employee Launched Projects)— Departments or groups of employees use their skills and energies to solve problems. Provides a way to respond to community needs in a small group environment.
- Honeywell Retiree Volunteer Program—Retired employee volunteers coordinate recruitment activities, organize and develop the programs, administer the office, and train and place other retired volunteers.

At Westinghouse every three years there is a "Community Involvement Survey" to determine the levels of employee participation. In 1981, 44 percent of the employees were active volunteers. Twenty-two percent of Westinghouse employees volunteered two to four hours per week, and 12 percent volunteered more than four hours a week.

Often community leadership is collaborative, as business executives join together to address social needs. The San Francisco Bay Area Business Leadership Task Force was established in 1982 when a group of Bay Area business leaders met to discuss ways in which the business community could become more active in community affairs. They were particularly concerned about regional employment trends and strategies, summer jobs for youth, and health-cost containment. They decided, after research into other collaborative efforts, that they should take the initiative in bringing together for-profit and nonprofit interests so that, with the leaders of community organizations, they could begin to devise new strategies to address these problems. The Task Force's report, "Rethinking Corporate Involvement: Some New Sector Roles in the Bay Area," notes that "Business cannot solve every local problem, but for some issues it can provide part of the solution by contributing to a new style of local problem solving that is collaborative, pragmatic and issue oriented."

In these and thousands of other cases, companies are finding ways to use their talent, experience, knowledge, facilities, money, trained people, and concern to support and strengthen the communities and causes with which they are involved.

Given the rapid and significant growth in the size and breadth of corporate public service, it is to be expected that some strains are evident. Some of these are internal, relating to the ability to manage the enterprise, and some are external, involving growing expectations and misunderstanding.

In my view, one of the more serious problems is the degree of significant understaffing that exists in corporate philanthropy. For more than ten years I've regularly visited private foundations and corporate grantmaking offices and have often been struck with how very much smaller the corporate staffs are. Other than some random inquiries and comments about this seeming disparity, I've never really focused on it. Lately, however, the dilemma of corporate efforts compared to staff capacity has seemed to reach crisis proportions, so I decided to test my impressions. I've now compared a random sampling of the staff sizes of approximately seventy-five private foundations and seventy-five corporate grantmakers. While I don't pretend that this has been a scientific study, I'm now absolutely satisfied that my impressions are borne out. In these 150 programs of equal grantmaking size, the private foundations have, on average, one professional staff person for each $1.2 million of grants, while the corporations have one staff person for each $2.3 million of grants, a ratio of approximately two to one. It is interesting that this ratio is about the same regardless of program size. For example, for programs awarding $10–$50 million in grants annually, private foundations have one staff person for each $1.44 million of grants and corporations have one staff person for each $3.26 million of grants; for programs in the $5–$10 million range, private foundations have one staff person for each $1.36 million of grants, while corporations have one staff person for each $2.30 million of grants; for programs in the $2–$5 million range, private foundations have one staff person for each $0.83 million of grants and corporations have one staff person for each $1.60 million of grants; and for programs under $2 million, foundations have one staff person for each $0.48 million of grants, while corporations have one staff person for each $1 million of grants. (For comparative purposes, I excluded community foundations, foundations with substantial operating programs, and corporations and foundations where the ratio seemed so extreme—high or low—as to suggest extraordinary circumstances.)

Some corporate grantmaking officials have pointed out that in addition to their professional staff, they are able to draw on other parts of the company for legal, computer, public relations, and other expertise, and that though this is hard to quantify, it needs to be taken into consideration in order to arrive at a more accurate comparison. Many foundations also engage outside consultants and other assistance not reflected in their staff sizes.

Even accounting for indirect staff services, the corporate operation would still probably be somewhere close to one-half that of the private foundation counterpart. This is compounded seriously when factors of complexity and volume (number of applications received and grants made) are factored in. The corporate operation is usually dealing with a program that is not limited to a few areas of concentration, such as the arts or human services; is dealing more often with many locations, such as plants or regional offices; has more diverse activities to manage, such as matching gifts and employee volunteering; and must be responsive to many more people inside and outside the company.

From my ten years as president of the National Council on Philanthropy and INDEPENDENT SECTOR, involving regular contacts with hundreds of foundations and corporate public-service operations, I'm convinced that the issue is decidedly *not* that private foundations are overstaffed. Most foundations are trying to do too much with too few people. Indeed, there is an unhealthy emphasis on keeping staff sizes small, particularly in the face of the kind of thoughtful judgment we expect donor organizations to exhibit. For corporations the disparity is serious, bordering on alarming.

The internal crisis suggested by inadequate staffing of a very public role is not unrelated to an understandable preoccupation on the part of CEOs and management with very real problems that are more immediate, such as takeovers and international competition, but the justifications for neglecting corporate public involvement cannot become routine. If the current crop of CEOs cannot or will not give high priority to how their organizations fulfill already staked-out roles in community service, serious doubts about corporate public service will be created and reinforced.

For many companies, the laudable effort to integrate public service into the mainstream of corporate life has some disadvantages. It has seemed logical, and indeed usually is, that public service should be related to other external responsibilities of the company, such as public affairs and public relations. In some cases, though, this integration causes contributions decisions to move too much toward self-interest and away from the crossroads of corporate *and* public interests. I've served as a consultant to companies where it was necessary to point out that, in an atmosphere of "everything must relate to the corporation's strategic plan," contributions decisions were being driven largely by public relations and government relations decisions. In some cases, for example, an increasing proportion of company giving is going to industry-related trade groups that are nonprofit but not charitable. The company's thinking is that what is good for their industry is good for the country. That may be so, but the costs should not come out of contributions.

Similarly, a few companies take from contributions budgets the funds that are used for cause-related marketing, or they increase marketing budgets for these efforts at the expense of contributions budgets. I'm all for anything that expands a corporation's public service, but decisions made for marketing reasons should be supported from marketing budgets.

A continuing quandary for corporations is whether to actively seek credit for contributions and other public service. In "Public Invisibility of Corporate Leaders," a fascinating piece in the *Harvard Business Review,* David Finn of Ruder and Finn lamented that corporations and their leaders don't get enough credit for what they do for society, and that out of a fear of criticism they don't make much of an effort to explain what they and their companies are doing for their communities and the nation. He concludes:

> I believe that executives have a great potential for inspiring leadership in contemporary society. But they need to let people see what kinds of human beings they are, what they believe in, what they want to accomplish through their business activities, and what values they want to achieve for society through their efforts. To accomplish these objectives, business executives with a talent for leadership should:
>
> 1. Integrate their communal and business lives so they can gain credit for their public services and be credible when making statements about their businesses.
>
> 2. Develop an appetite for being in the public eye as individuals who represent the character of their companies.
>
> 3. Speak publicly and convincingly about human needs and values as well as economic benefits when discussing business policies.
>
> 4. Have the courage to initiate company programs that grow out of their personal interests, and become the public spokesperson for those programs.
>
> 5. Develop their own sense of style about the conduct of their businesses without worrying that they may be catering to idiosyncratic tastes.
>
> 6. Persuade their stockholders that it is important for managers to be human beings who have deep concerns about the health and wellbeing as well as the material comfort and financial security of their fellow citizens.

The public may approve or condemn a specific corporate action, but if it knows what kind of person is responsible for the company's policies and what values he or she believes in, it is possible to be responsive to that leadership. Instead of being anonymous instruments of impersonal corporate interests, top executives can be understood as conscientious individuals doing their best to fulfill the responsibilities to society which they believe to be of great importance.

A statement released by the Business Roundtable in 1981 concluded that "all business entities should recognize philanthropy as good business and an obligation if they are to be considered responsible corporate citizens of the national and local communities in which they operate."

Reginald Jones, who served as head of the Business Roundtable and as chairman and CEO of General Electric, put the responsibility this way: "Public policy and social issues are no longer adjuncts to business planning and management. They are in the mainstream of it. The concern must be pervasive in companies today, from board room to factory floor. Management must be measured for performance in economic and non-economic areas alike and top management must lead."

One of the very best answers to whether it is the business of business to give anything away, and even whether such behavior works against the interests of stockholders, was provided by James Burke, chairman of Johnson and Johnson, when he and his company received the Advertising Council's 1983 Public Service Award. As reported in INDEPENDENT SECTOR's "Corporate Philanthropy," Burke said: "Those companies showed an annual 11 percent growth in profits compounded over 30 years! That happens to be better than three times the growth of the Gross National Product . . . which grew at 3.1 percent annually during the same period.

"If anyone had invested $30,000 in a composite of the Dow Jones 30 years ago, it would be worth $134,000 today. If you had invested the same $30,000 . . . $2,000 in each of these companies instead . . . your $30,000 would be worth over $1 million! . . . $1,021,861 to be exact!"

Burke closed by saying:

I have long harbored the belief that the most successful corporations in this country—the ones that have delivered outstanding results over a long period of time—were driven by a simple moral imperative—serving the public in the broadest possible sense—better than their competition.... We as businessmen and women have extraordinary leverage on our most important asset... goodwill... the goodwill of the public... if we make sure our enterprises are managed in terms of their obligations to society.... [T]hat is also the best way to defend this democratic, capitalistic system that means so much to all of us.

Corporate public service is getting bigger, broader, and tougher to manage, but the evidence is clear that companies that do it well, do well.

15
Guidelines for Giving

I HEAR REGULARLY FROM contributors who are uncertain about the best way to decide on donations. Some want to know how they can be sure an organization is legitimate. Others pour out their doubts as to whether most charities spend too much on fundraising. Finally, there are those who want to know how much anyone should be expected to contribute to charity.

For almost all inquiries, I can provide a positive orientation and some practical guidelines. First of all, in thirty-five years as a close observer of voluntary organizations, I have come across very few frauds. I am the first to condemn those who cheat in the name of charity—they are the worst of the worst—but for all that is sought and given, at least 99.9 percent is for legitimate purposes. When there is a scandal involving that remaining fraction of one percent, the news is just as big and negative as the charlatans deserve, but an impression that nobody can be trusted is created.

Column #1 of the same title from "The Voluntary Spirit," a collection of columns by Brian O'Connell. INDEPENDENT SECTOR, 1992.

When I ask people to analyze their own giving, almost everyone realizes that most of what they contribute goes to groups with which they are familiar. That, I tell them, is the largest source of their protection and assurance. Surveys of giving make clear that 95 percent of what we contribute goes to *our* church, *our* hospital, *our* college, and other institutions we know personally; or to organizations where we know some of the people involved, such as *our* local United Way, Cancer Society, museum, historical society, or hospice; or to international causes related to *our* local synagogue or church or to a branch of a national organization we know something about. For most of us, our contributions to those causes and organizations represent just about everything we give.

I know that many people worry or wonder whether even well-known groups do as much good as they could, and this is obviously harder to judge. Generally, I believe that organizations which operate in the public spotlight, compete in the marketplace for annual support, and involve volunteers for much of their energy and oversight are as scrutinized and well directed as any institutions in our society.

Senator Bob Packwood, who chaired both the Senate Commerce and Finance committees and therefore has had a good opportunity to observe all three sectors, says that on the basis of his regular dealings with government, business, and nonprofits, he finds that "voluntary organizations are by far the most reliable—that is, the most certain to do what they were established to do and what society expects of them."

Management consultant Peter Drucker was once asked by a business reporter, "What's the most effective organization with which you've ever worked?" The inquirer assumed that the answer would be a business corporation such as General Electric or Hewlett-Packard. Drucker thought a moment and replied, "The Girl Scouts." The reporter laughed and said he hoped Drucker would be willing to give a serious answer. Drucker responded that he was absolutely serious in believing the Girl Scouts to be the most effective group with which he had ever worked. He pointed out that if you take that many dedicated volunteers and complement them with a professional staff oriented and trained to increase the usefulness of volunteers, and you point all that energy and commitment toward an important social purpose such as the development of women and girls, those were clearly the ingredients for effectiveness and excellence.

Nonprofit organizations can and do learn a great deal from business about good management, bottom-line discipline, people development, evaluation of results, and much more, but these are not the only measurements of excellence, and every business is hardly the model of efficiency and effectiveness.

My basic response, then, to those who are worried about their donations is that almost all their support goes to organizations they know firsthand or in which they know some of the people involved, and that voluntary organizations are at least as reliable as other institutions in our society.

It's as we move from the known to the unknown that greater doubts are raised, but at least it helps to know that most of our concerns can be narrowed to a very small percentage of our giving. Most of us give to unknown appeals that stir us, and we hope the cause is all right. We are on less secure ground, but usually we're not gambling that much money, and from my experience the chances are good that the cause is okay. If we want to check more carefully, the attorney general in our state will probably have more information or can get it from the state where the organization is headquartered. Also, the local Better Business Bureau can often get information from its national Philanthropic Advisory Service. And there's a comprehensive service called the National Charities Information Bureau (19 Union Square West, 6th Floor, New York, NY 10003) that has reports on thousands of national appeals.

Even with all that backup, we have to realize that there is some risk involved when we send money to a cause we don't know much about, just as there is risk when we order merchandise from a company we don't know. That doesn't argue against doing either, but at least it does suggest that we shouldn't criticize a charity or a business when the transaction doesn't pan out. Never be afraid to ask for an organization's annual report, which should make clear who is involved and what the program and finances are, and if the organization won't provide it, beware.

When it comes to questions about how much each of us should give to the causes of our choice, five percent is the pretty basic measure. Increasingly, that's the standard for financial support. Obviously, the tithers who give 10 percent are the true leaders of our caring society, but we should all at least give five.

My summary message to those who inquire about contributing is so standard that it is even fixed in my secretary's word processor: "Don't punish yourself thinking you should respond to all the myriad requests that come your way. Target your giving to causes you care about and organizations you know firsthand or know indirectly through the people involved and you'll be on the safe side. Give at least five percent and you'll be doing your fair share."

16

For Voluntary Organizations in Trouble . . . Or Don't Want to Be

AFTER YEARS OF OBSERVING and trying to help organizations in trouble, I've gradually learned to recognize some of the danger signs and help volunteer and staff leaders face up to them.

From the opposite side, I've spent as many years marveling at organizations that are models of effectiveness and am finally able to understand and interpret what makes them so good.

This pamphlet draws on both experiences to assist organizations that are in trouble, or don't want to be, and to try to give a boost to all those which aspire to be the best.

"For Voluntary Organizations in Trouble . . . Or Don't Want to Be," by Brian O'Connell, INDEPENDENT SECTOR, 1993.

Danger Signs of Organizations in Trouble

When I'm asked to meet with the board or leaders of a nonprofit organization that describes itself in trouble, the difficulty invariably relates to one or more of these "at risk" stages or weaknesses.

Failure to Focus on Mission and Priorities

One of the first things I do when meeting with a board that is confused, troubled, or divided is to ask them to complete this sentence: "The mission of this organization is . . ." At that stage, I ask them not to discuss it or opt out of the assignment, but instead to write down their interpretation as best they can.

When those slips are turned in, I ask someone to put them on larger sheets of paper, and while this is taking place I ask the board members to finish this sentence: "The single most important thing the organization should accomplish this year is . . ." Again, I ask for no discussion or opting out. These answers are also transferred to larger sheets of paper and then both sets are put up on the wall.

And then I don't say a word.

After some minutes of looking over the mission statements and interpretations of priority activities, someone is almost certain to say something like "No wonder we're so mixed up!"

Ninety percent of the time, the difficulties faced by organizations in trouble relate to a failure to understand their mission or focus on their primary activities.

Failure to Invest in Building the Board

In *The Board Member's Book* and the related Nonprofit Management Series pamphlet on "Finding, Developing and Rewarding Good Board Members," I begin: "For the head of the board, having enthusiastic and reliable board members is almost as good as having an enthusiastic spouse and reliable children—and some days, such as just before the annual board meeting, you might trade the kids 2 for 1. The problem is that most of us wait until those moments of crisis to give adequate consideration to solid board membership. It's like trying to build a professional football team without the efforts of scouting, signing, training and rewarding. Our business is almost entirely people related, yet we invest almost nothing in people building. We get so tied up in today's needs that we don't reserve a realistic part of our resources for developing the talent and dedication necessary to carry and expand the association's efforts tomorrow. The building begins with the board itself."

Executive directors, board chairpersons, and directors will go on at length that the board doesn't include enough dedicated people, fundraisers, diversity, and so on, but when I inquire about the amount of effort invested in cultivating such people, the answer is almost always nil.

Sometimes the neglect is rationalized on the basis that every possible resource has to be invested in the organization's program, but I always counter that the program is hardly protected or advanced if the board is not functioning effectively.

Lack of Funds

If there is any one problem highlighted by organizations in trouble, it's lack of funds and fundraising capacity. Almost always, these organizations will point out that they are at least as deserving as other groups that are doing better but that somehow they just haven't been able to attract the needed support or the people capable of getting it.

In the chapter and pamphlet on fundraising, I state:

> The fundraising commitment must begin with the board and must be high on the agenda of a significant number of the trustees. Not only must it be of high priority but it must also be high in status and recognition within the organization. That's not easy. If you're wondering how to get moving, you probably already know the problem of a board of directors not really recruited with fundraising responsibilities distinctly in mind and if you are already getting most of your support from fees, contracts, or United Way, it's even harder to stir up real fundraising interest and urgency. Raising money takes dogged persistence, bullheadedness, salesmanship, year-round cultivation, board support and encouragement, a plan, an attainable goal,

and lots of excitement—to whit it's hard work. But if the board decides it's going to raise money and is willing to allocate at least 25 percent of its energy and resources to accomplish this goal, you can and will succeed.

Every time I'm asked by a board delegation if I think their organization can raise money, I repeat that they're in for some awfully hard work. I don't say this to discourage them. Indeed, I hope they'll push on, and I hope this applies to you. But if you're timid or your organization isn't really determined, you won't survive the obstacles, heartaches, and difficulties which, unfortunately, I can promise you lie ahead. On the other hand, if you have a cause that deserves support and you're willing to scratch, kick, and beg, you can raise money.

In recent years, years of enormous financial crisis for many voluntary organizations, I've met with at least seventy-five board and staff delegations seeking advice on development. I start with the same encouragement, but I also follow up quickly with how much work is in store. I emphasize that their organization must be prepared to devote at least 25 percent of its resources to fundraising and that the board head and chief staff officer will have to devote closer to 50 percent of their time for the first year or two. The reaction is rarely, "If that's what it's going to take, we'll do it!" Usually, the reaction is that it's unrealistic for an organization to devote that much time to fundraising. I'm sorry, but the reality is that to get started, or to reach a much higher level, that's what it takes. Stewardship is as much about building the capacity of an organization as it is about allocating resources wisely.

Confusion Between the Role of the Board and the Role of Staff

I've also observed that most organizations go into a temporary downturn when staff is first hired. The pattern is fairly typical. A wonderful group of dedicated volunteers, through their own individual efforts and without staff backup, have scrambled their way to having a significant program and are now at the point where they need and can afford some staff assistance. They hire a person and immediately the volunteers relax, turning much of the work over to the staff director. The volunteers assume the agency will be able to move forward.

In about a year, or at most two, the volunteers begin to view the scene with bewilderment; they find that the agency is doing less than it was before they hired staff and that it has lost much of its visibility and vitality. The volunteers will conclude that obviously the wrong staff was hired because more was being accomplished when the volunteers were doing it themselves. Before the downturn and discouragement become irreversible, the group's members may finally realize that they turned over far too much of the job to the staff and retreated to occasional approvals of staff actions, along with some irregular assistance to the poor bloke who is chairperson but who has begun feeling less and less responsible for the operation.

The worst illusion ever perpetrated in the nonprofit field is that the board of directors makes policy and staff carries it out. This is just not so. The board, with the help of the staff, makes policy and the board, with the help of the staff, carries it out. Unless volunteers are committed and involved in the action phase of the organization, the agency cannot develop and, in fact, should not be characterized as a voluntary organization. The staff exists to help the volunteers do the work of the organization. Staff members should not be expected or allowed to do most jobs directly. The greatest sinner in this respect is often the chairperson who turns over his or her responsibility to the executive director.

Deficits

An interesting list of objectives for good boards was put together by Michael Davis of the Rosenwald Fund. One of his best was "Face budgets with courage, endowments with doubt, deficits with dismay, and recover quickly from a surplus."

It's easy to get carried away with unduly optimistic income projections and unrealistic expectations, but the resulting deficits and the horror of budget cutbacks, particularly those which involve personnel, gradually should teach the lesson that it is better to face reality and disappointment during the budgeting process rather than later.

Income projections should be based on an objective analysis of *current* sources of income, including a source-by-source and gift-by-gift review. This not only makes for practical budgeting but also provides sensible preparation for the degree of work necessary to renew gifts and grants and to find new money. It's essential not to project substantial new income, or at least count on it, to cover fixed expenses. The usual approach for a nonprofit agency is to hope so desperately for new income that it gets counted in the budget; then, when it doesn't materialize, the group ends up with a deficit or facing horrendous cutbacks. The wiser approach is to have an opportunity for budget revisions during the year and/or allow additions according to new income actually produced.

The full board should be involved in approving the annual budget and should take this responsibility *very* seriously. Deficits are hell for everybody.

Confusion Between the Roles of the Chief Volunteer Officer and the Chief Staff Officer

In troubled organizations, I often find confusion, leading to strain and alienation, between the chief volunteer and chief staff officers. Organizations are particularly at risk when one of these two people leaves. Some chairpersons come from business backgrounds and tend to leave everything to staff, weakening the chair and the board. The next time around the new chairperson might come from an organization like the League of Women Voters, which often does not have staff, and therefore the volunteer leaders do it all and the board head may inadvertently take over the role of executive director. The problem today is compounded by the use of the term "chief executive officer" to describe either of the two positions, usually the staff director, but this title and the corporate model it represents rarely fit a vibrant voluntary organization.

I don't even use the term chief executive. It just doesn't describe the unique roles and relationship of chief volunteer and chief staff officer in a voluntary organization. The former must be active and effective, particularly in building the volunteer side of the organization. Committee heads, project chairpersons, and other officers are the chief volunteer officer's subordinates. They want to know what he or she thinks; they want to know where that person is going; and they want to know how what she or he considers important is to be done.

Most chairpersons assume that this kind of contact just happens; that the executive has somehow communicated all these things, or that a past chairperson has oriented a successor; or even that a person, simply by having been a member of the board, grasps new and larger responsibilities. There can't be cohesion in an organization without the chairperson's involvement in orientation and training and without his or her giving a great deal of thought as to how to effectively motivate, inspire, and stimulate persons who will be carrying the major part of the load.

A great deal of time and effort needs to be invested in being sure that the unique team of chief volunteer and chief staff officer understands and respects each other's roles and is working effectively together.

Confusion About the Role of Chief Volunteer Officer

Though this may seem to have been covered above, I give it special consideration because troubled organizations are often led, and poorly so, by people who don't really understand the role of the chairperson in building a sense of teamwork and confidence throughout the organization.

Several years ago one of my nominating committees recognized that a particular individual was the most deserving for selection as chief volunteer officer, but they were not going to select him because he was an absolute tiger in expressing opinions and putting other people down. The current chairperson felt that if the deserving individual really understood the difference between being an aggressive board member and being the chairperson the situation would change and agreed to provide orientation and mentoring for the individual if nominated. I never saw such a difference in performance. Instead of having a strong opinion on everything and expressing it stridently, the individual became a builder of confidence and people and turned out to be an absolutely first-rate leader. He acknowledged later that the difference was that he had never really thought about the job description and once he did he realized that he would have to behave very differently to succeed at it.

Confusion Between the Trusteeship Role of Board Members and Their Other Volunteer Roles

I've seen it happen repeatedly that board members and therefore staff will be terribly off balance because trustees don't feel sufficiently involved or are involved excessively in the wrong things. Gradually, I've learned that because volunteers are necessarily and appropriately involved in many of the day-to-day activities of the organization, including fundraising, annual meetings, program projects, and more, it's understandable that at the board table they often are not clear as to when they should be functioning as trustees and when they should be wearing their more general volunteer hats.

It's absolutely essential that the directors function quite literally as the trustees on matters of budgets, audits, evaluations, formal plans, hiring the executive director, and assessing performance, but these governance functions are usually only a relatively small part of a board meeting. Much of the time, board members are sitting not as trustees but rather as interested volunteers helping to think through public relations strategies, the building of annual meeting attendance, or assessing the effectiveness of a special event.

In these matters, boards, out of enthusiasm and concern, tend to function as extensions of committees and staff, but because they are at the board table they tend to make motions and decisions that seriously confuse who does what in the organization. It's inevitable that interested volunteer board members will become involved in such discussions. To try to make clear when the trustees are functioning in a governance role and when they are functioning as informed, but still informal, advisers to committees and staff, board agendas should be divided into governance matters that require trustee discussion and action and other matters on which the board might wish to provide opinions or be informed.

I've always been fascinated by how quickly serious problems within boards dissipate when the distinction between the trustee role of board members and their other volunteer functions is made clear.

The Problem of Trustees Who Are Single-Issue Advocates, or at Least not Trustees of the Whole Organization

Many boards tend to become divided when board members become champions of various parts of the organization (such as the research or library function), and woe to anybody who challenges that particular aspect of the association's work. It's natural that board members might have a special interest in and even a responsibility for certain parts of the organization, but it's essential that they be reminded of and function in their role as trustees responsible for the overall health of the organization.

I consulted recently with one of the largest voluntary organizations in the country and was surprised to find their board operating almost like a collection of armed camps, with virtually no one worrying about the good of the organization as a whole. Part of the solution was to add some at-large board members whose charge, at least for the first few years, will be to make certain that all directors are constantly reminded of their larger responsibility.

Boards and Staff Who Don't Know How to Deal With Dissent, or Are Protected From It

Sometimes the problem isn't contention but a lack of disagreement. In these organizations, things are ground into absolute mush before any action is taken, and if there is a difference of opinion it seems to threaten the organization's ability to function.

Don't be afraid of healthy controversy in boards and committees. If the cause is important, people will feel strongly about it, but not always in the same way. Let people debate, and even argue, but keep it within the bounds and context of the organization's mission. Don't be too quick to refer the issue to a committee or to try to mask very real differences.

Be sure that the board or committee is advised in advance, and exposed to all the necessary resource material, of items to be voted on. Try to be certain that the first time the issue comes forward the board has a chance to react and discuss it without being forced to take action. When the matter does come back, it will probably have profited from the board's discussion and the board will not feel as if it has been hurried into making a premature decision.

Once the board has acted, even if by split vote, the pattern should be to move on to the next item, with the losers accepting that they had a fair chance to express their contrary opinion. This is one of the key roles the chairperson should play in building the board team.

Organizations That Don't Evaluate Their Effectiveness, Adherence to Mission, Program Plan, and Priorities

Voluntary organizations are usually so busy doing that there isn't time—or it seems a poor use of time—to become involved with serious evaluation. Eventually, that will lead any organization into difficulty.

A medical researcher friend of mine, long active in voluntary organizations, has this wonderful description of how nonprofit groups generally evaluate their results: "Any group as bright as we are, and which has worked as long and hard as we have, must have done a lot of good."

Evaluation doesn't have to be complicated. It can be as basic as deciding what you want to achieve by the end of the year and then figuring out later if you got there. At its simplest, evaluation starts with an attainable goal to be accomplished at a realistic date, with a prior commitment to stop what you're doing on that date to see if your goal was actually achieved. The reason so many organizations don't follow this simple procedure is that they don't even start with a plan; therefore they don't have a specific goal or deadline to meet. Usually, fuzzy goals equal fuzzy evaluation, and unfortunately the combination usually adds up to fuzzy performance.

Failure to Hire the Right Executive Director

It's almost an axiom of voluntary organizations that the largest single task the board performs is to hire the executive director. Unfortunately, the job is very often done without anything like the investment it needs. Even when a careful job description is developed, along with identification of the type of person most likely to succeed in terms of personal attributes, skills, and experience, the search process is not really geared to screening that kind of individual. Someone who makes a good impression is often selected without careful checking of your needs against the candidate's qualifications.

It's particularly important that the outreach be very systematically pursued and that any serious candidates be interviewed and assessed using a checklist based on the job specifications and personal qualities desired.

I've had experience enough to predict that when this orderly method is used, boards will end up hiring someone who would not have been their first choice if left to their own instincts. I would further guess that most boards would agree later that their instincts would have deceived them.

Boards That Don't Carefully Evaluate Performance of the Chief Staff Officer, Including Setting and Defending Appropriate Compensation

It too rarely happens that the board of directors or the executive committee reviews an executive director's performance. Such review should be based on the job description and the executive director's role in assisting the board to carry forward the association's work. Most organizations overlook the need for an annual review and no evaluation is done until the point of brinkmanship is reached. The performance of the executive director should be measured in relation to the job description; to his or her effectiveness in working with the board to fulfill its priorities and establish accountability standards; and to his or her ability to contribute to expanded volunteer involvement and responsibility. The evaluation should take up a substantial part of a board or executive committee meeting. I don't believe that this critical responsibility should ever be delegated to a personnel committee.

The session should not be nitpicking, but it should be thorough enough so that if members have concerns about performance those issues will be raised and discussed objectively. At times, this process indirectly solves other relationship problems. A member of the board may be laboring under a misconception of the executive director's role or handling of a given situation, and once it's brought up the misunderstanding may be dispelled.

The chairperson should take time after the meeting to review the report, including items of commendation and areas for improvement. It should be a growth situation for the individual and therefore for the organization.

If the board's objective and fair evaluation of performance seems to suggest a mismatch, the executive director should be given an opportunity to make adjustments in performance, but if that isn't successful or just isn't likely, the board has to face up to it and get on with a search that will produce the right match.

At some point during the year, the board should also deal with the executive director's compensation. There should be a good deal of process involved, including being sure that the salary scale and benefits are competitive so that you're able to hold good people. It certainly is an "at risk" time for an organization when it loses a good chief staff officer.

Board members often think of staff salaries and related expenses as overhead. Even fairly sophisticated boards become concerned if staff salaries begin to represent a high proportion of the budget. Contrary to this view, I frequently counsel boards that unless the staff salaries and other supporting expenses come to more than 50 percent of the budget, the agency probably is not doing its job.

The basic program force in most citizen organizations is either: (1) the volunteers' time and energy, which moves the community toward improved attitudes and practices; or (2) the specialist staff members who provide direct service. The major cost involved in operating most voluntary organizations is the staff who provide day-to-day service to the volunteers or clients. The staff person serving a childhood mental illness committee or working to promote jobs for the handicapped is as legitimate a program expense as the nurse in a hospital, the teacher in a school, or the minister in a church. The staff is not overhead. I certainly agree that overhead should be kept as low as possible, and if the staff is spending most of its time on administrative activities, there is need for concern. But if staff time is logged on behalf of the mission of the organization, it is program money well spent.

Failure to Practice Openness and Full Disclosure

Some organizations that are functioning well get into trouble because their funders, the public, or regulators don't know enough to make an accurate judgment. In this day and age, voluntary organizations have to practice a considerable degree of openness and full disclosure to ensure that there is no suspicion or doubt about the way the organization is functioning and no lack of access to information by which people can make fair judgments.

Voluntary organizations enjoy distinct privileges such as tax-exemption and tax deduction of contributions and therefore bear a particular responsibility to comply with the public's right to know. The nonprofit organization that attempts to deceive the public or withhold information may be doing everything else right (though probably not), but it will receive little or no credit for the good it does if it loses the confidence of the public.

Failure to Live Up to Legal and Moral Responsibilities

The saddest situation by far for an organization and for the sector as a whole occurs when an organization is in trouble because it fails to live up to its legal and ethical responsibilities. INDEPENDENT SECTOR's report entitled "Ethics and the Nation's Voluntary and Philanthropic Community" stresses that "the public expects the highest values and ethics to be practiced habitually in nonprofit organizations. Those who presume to serve the public good assume a larger public trust." The report continues: "When our institutions do not reflect high standards of openness, honesty and public service, our contributors and clients feel ill-served, and because our organization depends on public goodwill and participation, if public support is eroded, so is our capacity for public service."

The primary level of ethical behavior relates to obeying laws such as being sure that required reports are submitted to government. However, most expectations, such as making the contributor's dollar go as far as possible for the client and the cause, are of a higher order. An organization must have processes by which it can decide whether the law is being obeyed, whether thoughtful ethics are being practiced, and whether tough ethical dilemmas are being openly considered and decided. Organizations that routinely utilize ethical decision-making practices will be much better prepared to handle a crisis when it hits.

INDEPENDENT SECTOR recommends that organizations have a code of ethics and that the board take the time at least once a year to examine whether the code is being practiced.

The IS report concludes: "Your organization should also do everything possible to be certain that the documents and the values they reflect become part of the culture of the total organization. For example, orientation sessions for new board members, staff and volunteers should include review of the code and other documents related to values, standards and ethical practices. All of these steps to develop and evaluate ethical practices should be seen as affirming the good an organization does and helping those involved with it to be proud of what they do."

Models of Effectiveness

At the beginning of this piece I mentioned that, though the emphasis should be on avoiding trouble, it is helpful to be aware of models of effectiveness and excellence. For five years INDEPENDENT SECTOR engaged in a large project designed to determine the characteristics of organizations that clients, funders, boards, peers, and others considered models of excellence. The results of that project, authored by project directors E. B. Knauft, Renee Berger, and Sandra T. Gray, have been published by Jossey-Bass as *Profiles of Excellence: Studies of Effectiveness of Nonprofit Organizations*. The authors summarized their findings:

> Picture a professional orchestra. Its musicians read notes proficiently, play their instruments well and practice long hours together. But it takes much more to turn a credible group of music makers into a world-class symphony orchestra.
>
> The same is true for a nonprofit organization. It takes more than a good board, a competent director and solid financial controls to differentiate the truly great organization from the larger universe of merely good ones. Our hallmarks of excellence are not substitutes for sound management practices. Rather, they are the *something extra* that makes all the difference.

Four overarching characteristics appear repeatedly in the best nonprofit organizations. These hallmarks [of excellence] reflect more than sound management practices, good staff and effective programs—although all are important components of excellence. But the very best groups consistently manifest something more—a clear and tangible *value added.*

The hallmarks of excellence in nonprofit organizations are:

(1) A clearly articulated sense of mission that serves as the focal point of commitment for board and staff and is the guidepost by which the organization judges its success and makes adjustments in course over time;

(2) An individual who truly leads the organization and creates a culture that enables and motivates the organization to fulfill its mission;

(3) An involved and committed volunteer board that relates dynamically with the chief staff officer and provides a bridge to the larger community; and

(4) An ongoing capacity to attract sufficient financial and human resources.

The book examines in detail each of these "hallmarks" and provides case studies of organizations that became excellent because of them.

One quick way to look at your organization might be to match it against a profile I developed after years of trying to figure out why some voluntary organizations fail and others succeed. The successful ones have these characteristics:

- a cause worth getting excited about;
- an ability to generate funds to do the job;
- programs that in fact do something for the cause;
- adequate attention to morale in order to keep the undertaking spirited and vigorous, even when the immediate tasks are not;
- an appropriate emphasis on increasing the number of citizens involved;
- an ability to keep the volunteers in charge, even after the operation is staffed;

- the flexibility to respond effectively to new problems and opportunities and to fit the profile of "ad-hocracy," which must increasingly characterize the useful organization;
- a capacity to keep the real mission in focus no matter how frenzied things become or how great the pressure to move into new areas. This means that all important decisions are made with the organization's "reason for being" kept clearly in the forefront.
- the vision to see beyond the horizon, along with a sensitivity to human needs and an almost contradictory toughness to build an organization capable of translating that vision and sensitivity into change.

Whether you're trying to get your organization out of trouble, to avoid trouble, or to move it toward excellence, keep in mind that those who struggle on behalf of important causes open themselves to frustration and disappointment. But through and after it all, those times of making things happen for the better are among our lasting joys. Hang in there.

17

The Role of the Board and Board Members

An interesting list of objectives for the ideal board member, attributed to Michael Davis of the Rosenwald Fund, has endured for more than fifty years. Here are five of his best:

> Know why the organization exists, and annually review why it should.
>
> Give money, or help get it, or both.
>
> Face budgets with courage, endowments with doubt, deficits with dismay, and recover quickly from a surplus.
>
> Interpret the organization's work to the public in words of two syllables.

Adapted from Chapter 4 of *The Board Member's Book*, by Brian O'Connell. New York: The Foundation Center, 1985. Revised edition, 1993.

> Combine a New England sense of obligation with an
> Irish sense of humor.

Boards of directors differ according to the organization's size and age; whether it functions as a federation or a single institution; whether it has staff; and whether it is a service organization with the board having ultimate authority, or a cause-oriented association where the membership body shares responsibility.

There are some universal truths applicable to every nonprofit organization, beginning with legal responsibility. Whether as board members you are called trustees, directors, governors, or something else, you are in essence trustees in the literal and legal sense of the term. No matter how the organization is structured or to what degree authority is delegated to staff, committees, or affiliates, the board and therefore the trustees are ultimately accountable.

In a 1984 court action in New Jersey involving an organization called Friends of Clinton Hill, a sympathetic judge listened to the board members' reasons for not knowing that their association had failed to pay the government for income taxes withheld and social security. The judge described these volunteers as "selfless," "dedicated," and "compassionate," but said nevertheless that the law left him no alternative but to hold them accountable for all such taxes as well as stiff interest penalties.

Whether it is a service agency or a cause-oriented membership association, the board has the principal responsibility for fulfillment of the organization's mission and the legal accountability for its operations. Usually the bylaws stipulate something like "the affairs of the corporation are vested with the board." There have been several legal cases where board members were held legally accountable, largely because they failed to exercise reasonable oversight and objectivity. When those cases are reported in the newspapers, the trustees are often quoted as "not having seen financial reports," "not having known," "not aware that the organization had contracted with a firm owned by one of the staff or board members," or in other ways making clear that the trustees did not take responsibility for knowing what was going on.

The law, however, is fair as long as the trustee's attention to responsibility is reasonable. Joseph Weber, former head of the Greater New York Fund, pointed out in "Managing the Board of Directors" that "this does not mean that a director needs to fear liability for every corporate loss or mishap that may occur. On the contrary, a Director is generally protected from liability for errors of judgment as long as he or she acts responsibly and in good faith, and with the basic interests of the corporation as the foremost objective."

Although the legal responsibility is real, and some boards and agencies are highly complex, the role of the board should still be seen in the fairly simple framework of "What have we trustees agreed to be accountable for?"

I have been through hundreds of books, pamplets, and training manuals relating to boards of directors and find that most of them try to deal with bylaws, recognition, and other specifics before or even in lieu of dealing with the basic question of what they are accountable for. I find it helpful to start with the standards of performance by which organizations are held accountable and then work backward to see how the board can be sure that the organization passes those tests.

Two groups have worked for years to develop and summarize the basic standards for voluntary organizations: the National Charities Information Bureau (NCIB) and the Philanthropic Advisory Service of the Council of Better Business Bureaus (CBBB).

It's revealing that both standard-setting bodies emphasize the role of the board itself. Although it may seem simplistic to say that the first role of the board is to be sure that the board is fulfilling its role, that's often the last place where accountability is exercised. Board members blame staff, committees, the fundraising chairman, the treasurer, and everyone else for failures in the operation, but rarely take a look at whether the board itself meets the kind of standards laid down for boards by the NCIB and CBBB.

In "Major Challenges to Philanthropy," a paper commissioned by INDEPENDENT SECTOR, Robert L. Payton, former president of the Exxon Education Foundation and later director of Indiana University's Center on Philanthropy, put it on the line:

As a group, it is the trustees who are most important in protecting the standards of philanthropy. If you smile at that, knowing from our own experience of trustees whose ignorance or single-mindedness made them part of the problem rather than part of the solution, I also smile—but in pained discomfort. Like it or not, the trustees are the structural bulwark defending the public interest in philanthropy. And if I'm right about that, then the education of trustees claims a very high priority on our collective agenda.

At its core, the board's job is to be sure that the organization measures up to standards, not just as an evaluator but also as the group responsible for seeing that the organization develops the capacity to meet those standards. Trustees can't sit back and be the high court or critic; likewise, trustees can't hide behind the myth that it is the board's responsibility to make policy and the staff's responsibility to carry it out.

Imagine for a moment the board's role if the organization did not have a staff. If an association were run entirely by volunteers, the accountability would be much clearer. One can't just make decisions and then walk away without being sure those decisions are translated into practice and results.

In a helpful publication entitled "Trustee Responsibilities" published by the Association of Governing Boards, John W. Nason lists twelve functions. Although they are written for educational institutions, they are applicable to almost all nonprofit organizations. To that end, I've taken the liberty of substituting the title of chief staff officer for president.

- appointing the chief staff officer
- supporting the chief staff officer
- monitoring the chief staff officer's performance
- clarifying the institution's mission
- approving long-range plans
- overseeing the program
- ensuring financial solvency
- preserving institutional independence
- enhancing the organization's public image

- interpreting the community to the organization
- serving as a court of appeal
- assessing board performance

These functions are similar to those performed by the board of directors of a business corporation, but in many ways the nonprofit organization depends far more on its board for fulfillment of its goal. Indeed, the smaller the organization, the greater is the dependence on volunteer performance.

Kenneth L. Dayton, former chief executive officer of Dayton Hudson, serves on many corporate, foundation, and large and small voluntary agency boards and has this to say about the similarities and differences in the boards' responsibilities:

> It is my experience that a board's role in the governance of nonprofit organizations—both philanthropic and voluntary—is exactly the same as it is in for-profit corporations.
>
> This covers moral and legal responsibility, strategy determination, allocation of resources, goal setting, evaluation of performance, rewarding and motivating management, making the tough decisions on top personnel, and being willing and available to assist in the areas of special experience. (It also involves strengthening the board itself—determining criteria for membership and setting policies for tenure and rotation.)
>
> Those board roles are absolutely essential to the effectiveness of all public corporations—profit and non-profit. Contrary to popular notion, I've found that it is often on the nonprofit side that boards take those responsibilities most seriously.

Dayton's last point about the degree of responsibility exercised by volunteer trustees contradicts other perceptions, but if one thinks about it, although the businessperson serving as an outside director of a corporation might take that responsibility seriously in terms of prestige, attendance, and legal liability, he or she really knows that the trustee's role means far more to the success of the institution in the voluntary world. A business corporation obviously needs its board for legal and practical reasons, but it isn't nearly so dependent on those individuals for its income and community outreach. Nor is it likely that corporate board members serve on the sales, marketing, and manufacturing committees as they do on the nonprofit organization's rehabilitation, fundraising, and public relations committees.

Perhaps even more important is the degree to which voluntary organizations look to individual trustees for leadership. Beyond participation and the essential procedures it institutes to ensure accountability, the board of the nonprofit organization has a substantial but rarely defined responsibility and opportunity for leadership.

The National Charities Information Bureau distributes an extensive checklist under the heading "What a Good Board Member Does"; it's significant that the first point is, "inspires and leads."

Usually when we think of leaders and leadership, we envision the towering giant who can do anything or the charismatic magician who can get the rest of us to do anything. In "A Guide For New Trustees," from the Association of Governing Boards, Nancy Axelrod quoted a *Wall Street Journal* article that described the ideal board member as "a man or woman with the versatility of Leonardo da Vinci, the financial acumen of Bernard Baruch, and the scholarly bent of Erasmus."

Most leadership actually comes from ordinary people who have it in them and rise to responsibility. These people are all around us, leading thousands of community and national institutions through conviction, hard work, and a quiet ability to help individuals and organizations realize their own roles and worth.

In all the resource materials I've reviewed, most of the experts enumerate the kinds of professional experience an organization will need on the board and pay no attention to personal qualities. But when I look at what makes a board tick, it's often the ability to work together that counts. Cyril O. Houle, in his book *Governing Boards,* writes: "Organization is merely the way by which people relate themselves to one another so as to achieve their common purposes."

In *The Volunteer Board Member in Philanthropy,* the NCIB lists the qualities of good board members. Such members:

> 1. are dedicated to helping others and modest in the light of their responsibilities as board members;

2. approach their responsibilities in the spirit of a trustee on behalf of contributors, their intended beneficiaries, and the public at large;
3. stand up for their convictions, even at the cost of misunderstandings or disapproval in their business or social life;
4. back up other board members and staff, rising to their defense when they are unjustly criticized or attacked;
5. treat staff as a partner in a high calling, maintaining overall supervision and control but not interfering with day-to-day administration;
6. avoid being overawed by others on the board, whether they be executive staff; tycoons of business, labor, or society; or professionals in social work, education, medicine, etc.;
7. welcome information and the best available advice, but reserve the right to arrive at decisions on the basis of their own judgment;
8. respect the right of other board members and staff to disagree with them and to have a fair hearing of their points of view;
9. accept as routine that decisions must be made by majority vote and that they will at times go against one or more members;
10. criticize, when necessary, in a constructive way, if possible suggesting an alternative course;
11. recognize that time and energy are limited and that over-commitment may prove self-defeating;
12. endeavor to keep disagreements and controversies impersonal and to promote unity; and
13. maintain loyalty to their agency, within a higher loyalty to the welfare of the community and humanity as a whole.

I've been through enough board orientation and training sessions to know that many newer board members are frustrated, even exasperated, and want to shout, "But you still haven't told me what I'm supposed to do!"

On the most basic level, you, as a board member, should understand the mission of the organization, attend board meetings, serve actively on at least one committee, be certain that you and the board as a whole are in control of planning and evaluation, contribute to a sense of camaraderie and teamwork, and ask questions.

At least half of those board members who wanted me to say exactly what they should do are now exclaiming, "That doesn't seem enough!" If it's any help, I can pretty much guarantee that if you'll do those things, the rest will become obvious.

Most lists of fundamentals refer to the trustee's role in raising money. The veteran fundraiser Harold Seymour used to put it bluntly: "Contribute wealth, wisdom and work." Today, in our efforts to be more representative, it's not fair to put the arm on everybody for $10,000, or even $500. On the other hand, I think it is fair to ask all board members, within their means and spheres of contacts, to contribute as much as they can and to help raise money. Asking for this help should be the responsibility of other volunteers and not the staff, and no board member should feel above these obligations.

Just a word on another basic responsibility, involving the importance of asking questions. If you don't understand the financial statements or the budget or the issue being voted on, ask questions. Sometimes these are better asked ahead of time or during the break so that you are not taking up too much time, and you can use these opportunities to get a bit of tutoring in areas where you are not as knowledgeable as others. However, the ultimate and necessary task is to understand what you are voting on. I can absolutely guarantee that other trustees will be grateful that someone else admits to being confused, and that this will lead to a greater sense of comfort in asking other questions. If you are accountable and don't understand it, where does that leave you and the organization?

There is a balance between not being intimidated into activity and at the same time not feeling guilty if you don't understand everything. Pick the areas that really seem important and on which others don't seem to be forthcoming. Don't be critical of yourself or others because you or they don't seem to understand or have an interest in everything. It's not realistic to expect that all board members will have an interest in or a grasp of all the things the organization is doing. My experience is that voluntary agency boards of any size are rarely composed of individuals who have across-the-board interest or knowledge. I find that if a board is effectively organized, some members will have an intense interest in certain topics and others will have a like interest in other issues, and that, in total, the group will provide an effective forum for a reasonable discussion of all the issues.

Boards tend to build and perpetuate more structure than is necessary, thus obscuring comprehension and accountability. You don't have to reach the point of needing a committee on committees to know that too much time is going into organization. It's amazing how quickly organizations become occupied with committee structure, involved procedures, and complicated lines of authority, to the point where they end up serving their structure and not their mission.

The structure of a service agency can be a good deal simpler than that of a federation or cause-oriented association that has a large voting membership and many affiliates. The latter may need a far larger board that is more representative of many constituencies, and the board will need to be extremely careful in the division of activities and power as it relates to the voting membership, delegate assembly, or whatever the larger group is called. On the other hand, the smaller board related to the service organization has the disadvantage of not having the larger groups to draw on for proven leadership. And while it has the advantage of simpler structure and lines of authority, it will pay a price in limited outreach. Thus, the board members for the service organization must be chosen very carefully to compensate for the shortcomings in outreach, experience, representation, and proven commitment. The importance of this factor is compounded by the small size of the board, which makes each seat on it count all the more.

Because of size and fewer opportunities to come up through the ranks of the organization, attendance at board meetings is all the more important in the service operation. It's also necessary in order to build a sense of responsibility. People will come into the organization without much prior exposure or sense of continuity and will be inclined to be passive and a bit too respectful of the leadership. It's helpful to realize that, on the surface, the board will seem less important because the staff is so much in charge, but you will need to overcome that perception and work all the harder at building a sense of responsibility and participation.

Whatever the kind of board, don't be afraid of healthy give and take. Among other things, it builds a sense of family. Board meetings should be viewed as arenas for controversy. If the issues are laid out in advance, are well formulated, and are clearly presented, and if sufficient time is available for debate, then it is healthy and constructive for board members to question, debate, and disagree.

One of the common faults of nonprofit organizations is that their leaders too often strive for compromise and unanimous votes. My experience has been that if you are dealing with real issues, striving too hard for compromise and unity may mean that you are not squarely facing the issues themselves, or you don't have the right mix of people, or you've watered down the issues until they're meaningless. It's far healthier to have a split vote as long as the issues are on the table, the debate is fair, and there has been sufficient time for consideration.

Providing for fair and objective consideration is easier said than done. Those in charge of the meeting often have strong feelings about the issues, meetings are usually too short for any real discussion, and there is too little advance dissemination of the facts to prepare people for adequate debate and an informed vote.

If there is a significant controversy, the organization must take the time to present the issues before the board so that the matter can be decided without creating the feeling that something has been put over on people. There will always be the temptation to slip a touchy matter through to avoid hurt feelings or ill will, or to let the executive committee handle a matter simply because it is potentially upsetting. Don't tolerate any of it. Be absolutely certain that a proper process is available and that this process is objectively and fairly followed to the letter.

It is far better to lose even on critical issues as long as the organization comes out of the battle with greater confidence in the integrity of the process. It's also better to take additional time for debate on major items than to put them behind you. On major issues, I always suggest that, initially, the matter should come up for discussion without a vote, even if this means postponement. It is more conducive to correct decision-making and to confidence in the system to take the extra time for consideration and review. Even on lesser matters, I generally favor having the board consider issues at one board meeting for a vote at the next. Committee chairmen and staff members are almost always dismayed when I recommend this process. Usually they have worked hard on a project, on guidelines, or on a position statement, and they feel it's imperative that the vote be taken as soon as possible. My approach is that if the matter is important, it's worth being sure that people know the issues. I also believe that by following this course there is more likely to be fellowship once the vote is taken.

The posture of the leader should be one of patience, tolerance, and flexibility. I include flexibility because leaders will often have their own biases, and yet they especially must be willing to seek out and really listen to new facts and different opinions. The more important the issue, the more intense the feelings and debate are apt to be. You will find that some people dig in their heels very early and are adamant about a given position. You will also find that people tend to describe the issues as a matter of principle or moral right. Generally, if you look closer, you will find they have confused policies with principles, or regulations with philosophy. It's helpful to delineate the important distinctions among philosophy, principles, policies, procedures, rules, and regulations. It's easier to take something lower on the totem pole too seriously simply by confusing it with a higher value.

Although this will not apply to the majority of readers, it is important to say something about the national board of an association with local chapters. It doesn't matter whether the national operation is organized as a corporate headquarters or the hub of a federation; it will still be the central entity and as such must provide dynamic leadership for the total organization. This includes responsibility for the organization's spirit, direction, thrust, policies, and guidelines.

One basic way to reduce built-in tensions and to keep the national level attuned to local needs is to be sure that the national board of directors is composed overwhelmingly of people who come from the affiliates. Even if your organization operates as a tight national corporation, there can't be correct decision making and follow-through without local volunteers playing a substantial role in making the decisions. On the national level, the organization should be largely peopled and run by individuals who have current, or at least recent, experience on the firing line. The affiliates must feel it's their national association or, regardless of how dynamic the leadership is, there won't be followership.

Even if you achieve the ultimate in representation, don't expect that harmony will automatically follow. You will still have to work hard at it. Remember Pogo's discovery: "We have met the enemy and he is us."

The object of all the lessons to minimize friction and create unity is to use the wonderful volunteer energy and time to fight for the cause and not against one another.

That's a pretty good rule for the role of all boards and board members.

18

The Board's Biggest Decision: Hiring the Chief Staff Officer

SELECTION OF THE CHIEF staff officer of a nonprofit organization is clearly the most important decision the board makes, but this responsibility is often handled poorly. It's my experience, born of many sad lessons, that it takes a particular type to succeed in the staff role in a voluntary or philanthropic agency. Over the years, I've developed a profile that helps me screen persons who are exploring staff possibilities. My current profile of the persons most likely to succeed reads as follows:

Excerpts from Part 6, "Recruiting, Encouraging and Evaluating the Chief Staff Officer," of the nine-part Nonprofit Management Series, by Brian O'Connell. Part 6 is adapted from Chapter 8 of *The Board Member's Book*, by Brian O'Connell. New York: The Foundation Center, 1985. Revised edition, 1993.

- They're committed to public service. This is more than a generalization. The persons who succeed will face many rocky times. They'll be underpaid for their ability and they'll have to put up with a great deal of conflict. For these reasons and many more, they must have a dedication to public service that will get them through the tough times.
- They like people and get along well with them. Liking people is often used as the only criterion for selection and therefore can be exaggerated. In carrying responsible positions in voluntary agencies, however, most staff people deal with a wide variety of individuals and must be able to get along with them.
- They can subordinate their personal needs and preferences to the needs and goals of the organization. This requirement eliminates the majority of candidates. Most of us cannot consistently subordinate our needs, aspirations, and satisfactions. But the really successful staff person in the volunteer agency must have this capacity.
- They have a great deal of patience and tolerance. Staff persons work with a variety of volunteers who are often at their most excitable pitch. The more vibrant and active an agency, the more this will hold true.
- They are mature. Psychologists define maturity as the ability to forego short-term satisfactions in favor of long-term goals. This applies to organizations as well as to individuals and particularly to successful staff persons. Most goals are long-range and require persistent, dogged pursuit through all kinds of difficulties. The satisfactions are rarely found on a weekly or even monthly basis. It's only as the agency looks back from a fuller perspective that the attainments are visible and the satisfactions present.
- They're willing to work hard. Successful people usually work hard, and this is particularly true in the nonprofit field. There is so very much to be done, the dedication of the volunteers is so high, and the

number of forces to be dealt with so great that the only way to achieve success is by working awfully hard.

A Demonstrated Capacity

Search committees must recognize the size of the recruiting job. Despite general acknowledgement that recruitment of the staff head is the most important decision the board will make, recruitment is often almost casually approached. As a result, persons who are not really qualified are often selected.

A committee should be appointed by the board of directors. It is essential that a majority of the committee be composed of board members, but it can also include an able staff person or two from other agencies in the community. If there is a parent organization, a key volunteer or staff person from that group should also serve. The first task of the committee is to decide on the skills and attributes desired. These will constitute a checklist for later interviewing and should immediately be translated into a job description, salary scale, and even advertisements if these are to be used.

Since most people do not fit the profile of success, it is extremely difficult to find those people most likely to succeed. I've found that the simplest way to solve this problem is to locate someone who has already demonstrated a capacity to succeed in the milieu. For this reason, I repeatedly and doggedly advise search committees to look within the nationwide group with which they are affiliated for experienced or promising people. If that doesn't apply in your case, then I advise checking with agency directors in your area. In other words, do almost anything to find candidates who have already demonstrated a capacity to succeed in this kind of work.

I am often told that it's better to locate a person who knows the local scene. I don't believe it. A bright, effective community organizer is going to get acquainted with that scene and develop contacts in lightning-fast time.

By the time you've developed your list of skills and attributes, you'll be overwhelmed by the realization that the person you need will have to be mature, very experienced, and brilliantly able. This, in turn, will suggest an older person. But the experience of many agencies, and certainly the experience of the Peace Corps, VISTA, the Office of Economic Opportunity, and other groups, makes clear how quickly a young, dedicated person can learn and how much this dedication means to achieving success.

You may find that you want to do some advertising. This can be done through newspapers, organization newsletters, and professional journals. Use newspaper advertising only when you have not been able to come up with enough candidates by close examination of personnel rosters in the organization and by talking to other agency executives.

One last word of caution. Beware of the board member who has a friend. More agencies make bad decisions because search committees find it awkward to decide against the friend of the president or a person pushed hard by a board member. The smaller the community, the tougher this is. The goal should be to hire the best possible person. The positive results of doing that will outweigh any short-term awkwardness.

Screening and Interviewing

- Screen the résumés down to five to ten people and have someone take a personal look at each candidate. If a prospect resides in another city, ask your sister organizations to take a look at the candidate or involve your board members who travel. Members of your board may have counterparts in that city, which at least gives you an opportunity to know whether the person seems to live up to his or her résumé.
- When the group is narrowed down, do some extensive reference checking. I don't put much stock in listed references, although I do contact them and ask pointed questions. I put much more stock in my telephone conversations with past supervisors. I've learned the hard way that most references and supervisors want to be helpful to the candidate, if only to be rid of him or her. Accept that this can be the case and work very hard to get the facts. Make clear how much you are counting on the supervisor's

candor. One of the points I make is that even if the person is hired, I want to know what skills or attributes will need strengthening. This is not only truthful and helpful, it is often the key to opening up a discussion of possible weaknesses.

- I'm often on the other side of these reference calls, and, with very few exceptions, I am appalled at how cursory the review is. As a consequence, I rarely have to be as candid as I would be if the questioning were sharp. This tells me that most people have made up their minds but still want to go through the steps of clearance without having their decision shaken. My approach is to shake the daylights out of my judgment. I'd rather face the error at that stage than when the person is on the job.

- Do a thorough credit check on your finalist(s). Often the current supervisor won't know a person's credit problems. The last thing you want is to bring a poor credit risk into your job and town. I've known of several public scandals that shook association reputations that could have been avoided by a simple credit check.

- Some candidates stipulate that no reference checking can be done. They make the legitimate case that they are simply looking into a situation and until they are sure they want to apply, they would rather not stir things up. At times you will have to abide by their wishes. Have it understood, however, that if a person does become a finalist, the checking will have to be done before anything is firmed up. I have learned over the years that the majority of people don't succeed in this field; consequently, there are many inefficient people in it, quite a few of whom compensate for their generally low level of performance by excelling at selling themselves in job interviews.

- The full search committee should see the candidates, if possible, during the same day, or on successive days. The group should take the time to decide how they'll conduct themselves during the interviews. The committee should develop a list of skills and attributes and clear any revisions in the job description and salary scale with the board of directors.

- Don't play games during the interview; don't try to shake up the candidate or try other ways to "see what the candidate is really made of." That's a good way of turning off your best candidates. Conduct the interview as a straightforward, candid discussion of the job and the candidate's strengths and weaknesses. The goal is to objectively determine whether there is a match or a potential mismatch between the job description and the candidate. It's useful to describe real-life situations in the organization and to ask the candidate, almost as though he or she were an organization consultant, to share ideas for dealing with those situations.

- It's important, too, to candidly explain any reservations the committee has about the individual in terms of gaps in experience, possible weak areas, a questionable reference check, and the like. Remember that it's a two-way proposition. Help the candidate to screen him or herself out. If the selection process is strung out at all, keep the candidates posted. This is a courtesy too often overlooked.

- Naturally, the committee's own instincts will play a significant part in the final recommendation. It is advisable, however, to introduce some objective measures in order to check your intuition and to be certain that each candidate is being viewed in light of the same criteria. My suggestion to search committees is that they take the attributes and skills needed and set out a score sheet. Use a rating of zero to five for each skill and personal attribute, with five being the highest mark. It's a good idea not to use these score sheets during the interview, but, instead, to take a few minutes after each interview for the committee members to mark their score cards. Seeing all candidates on the same day, or on successive days, will bring more uniformity into this process.

- After rating the candidates, the committee will probably be surprised at the scores. You will be fascinated by the fact that some candidates who didn't seem very impressive scored well. This, in turn, will lead to a much more objective discussion of the candidates in relation to the skills and attributes you are looking for. One individual may not be terribly dynamic but may score solidly right across the board. You may still decide on the individual who has more flair, but, again you may not. It's the scoring that will lead you to know what you're deciding.

I have had experience enough to predict that when this more orderly method is used, the committee members will end up hiring someone who would not have been their first choice if left to their own instincts. I would further guess that they would agree then and two years later that their instincts, to some extent, had deceived them.

Final Selection

The search committee reports to the board. If it is not possible for the full board to be involved in the decision, the executive committee usually has that authority. Some organizations give the search committee final authority to identify one choice and then refer the candidate to the board of directors or executive committee. I tend to favor the search committee narrowing the field to two to four people and then having the board or executive committee do the final interviewing. When the process involves the full board or executive committee, the most experienced people are participating. This also means that the larger group will have a real commitment to the candidate selected.

Follow a strict timetable for selecting an executive director. Prolonged search operations are unhealthy for the organization's morale and are unnecessarily awkward. At the local level the process should not require more than three months, including time to determine attributes and skills, develop the job description and salary scale, and search for and screen applicants.

Please do send letters to the references, prior supervisors, and present employers of the person selected. This is a courtesy almost always overlooked but one that will help your own public relations. The president or chairperson of the search committee should call the other finalists to thank them for their participation and to briefly explain the final decision. Let the candidates ask questions about the impression they made. This can be useful to them in future situations.

19
Compensation in Nonprofit Organizations

COMPENSATION IN THE nonprofit sector represents four very different problems:

First, some salaries and other compensation arrangements are egregiously high.

Second, some compensation arrangements appear to be high because too little effort has been made to interpret what it takes to attract and hold people who can lead large and complex voluntary institutions.

Third, there is an incorrect but pervasive interpretation that salaries are overhead.

Fourth, and most severe, most salaries and benefits in nonprofit organizations are so low as to threaten the development and maintenance of essential activities.

All four problems require urgent attention.

"Compensation in Nonprofit Organizations," by Brian O'Connell. Washington, D.C.: INDEPENDENT SECTOR, 1993.

For the first, involving the high flyers, it is essential to the integrity of the independent sector that there be acknowledgement and intolerance of unconscionable compensation. Physicians who buy up the income streams for such departments as radiology and pathology in charity hospitals and thereby profit annually from nonprofit endeavor to the tune of half a million dollars or more are terrible models of charitable behavior. It is also disheartening to learn about salaries, perks, and expense accounts in other charitable organizations that stretch even the most extreme interpretation of what is reasonable and necessary.

For the second problem, involving what appears to be high compensation but may in fact be reasonable and necessary, the saddest lesson in all of the recent disclosures is how many board members readily admit that they were not involved with setting salaries, don't even know what the compensation is, and are the first to run for cover. These very boards are where the solutions must begin.

Boards must be involved in setting compensation. They are trustees in the legal sense and stewards in the moral sense. As representatives of the community and/or the affiliates, the trustees must grapple with decisions about salaries and other compensation to the end that they agree what is right and are prepared to defend it. In INDEPENDENT SECTOR, every three years the board, in what I gather are awkward debates, sets the limits of my compensation, leaving to the management committee the annual review of my performance as long as there is a report back to the board on any adjustments made. Corporate directors think my salary is low and community activist directors believe it is high, but they are all representatives of our members, who pay the bills, and, therefore, they have to work it out.

In the current storm about nonprofit salaries, my compensation has been willingly reported and the board is the first to step forward to explain it. My salary is high compared to those in some organizations of similar size, but the board has taken into consideration the unique and complex nature of INDEPENDENT SECTOR and has adjusted and defended my compensation accordingly.

On the third dilemma, boards, regulators, and others constantly make the mistake of assuming that salaries are, per se, overhead. Actually, the staff person serving a childhood mental illness committee or working to promote jobs for the disabled is just as legitimate a program expense as a nurse in a hospital, a teacher in a school, or a minister in a church. I certainly agree that overhead should be kept as low as possible, and if the staff is spending most of its time on fundraising or management activities, there is need for concern. But if staff time is logged on behalf of the mission of the organization, it is program money well spent.

The basic solution is for nonprofit organizations to add to their required financial reports a functional spreadsheet, which reflects allocation of time reports and other costs to assigned program, management, and fundraising functions, so that boards, contributors, and others can see at a glance exactly how the total resources are used.

At the fourth level, involving inadequate salaries and benefits, the problems and solutions are the most serious. As crucial as it is to deal with the first three problems, the even larger test of our commitment to public trust involves building the long-term capacity of nonprofit organizations. At the heart of that solution is the ability to attract and hold staff who have the talent and stamina to deal with the needs of their communities.

Overshadowed by the tiny proportion of the highly paid are the vast majority of associations, including congregations, whose people are so inadequately compensated that all but the most dedicated leave through exhaustion or better offers. Salaries in nonprofit organizations are approximately two-thirds those of comparable jobs in government, and at the entry level they are likely to be only one-half, which sets up enormous barriers to attracting able young people in the first place.

In social welfare operations that deal with the most vulnerable in our society, providing such essentials as food, shelter, and job placement, benefits are scant to nonexistent, and even where they are provided they are rarely portable from one agency or even one affiliate to another.

Despite our need to deal with all the other problems relating to compensation, we must not be diverted from addressing the most fundamental challenge, which requires investing in the sector's capacity to be of even greater service to people, communities, and causes.

Salaries are a means to that end and the extremes of compensation must never be allowed to become the end of the means.

20

The Common Sense of Sabbaticals or Project Leaves

IN 1976, AFTER TEN years as executive director of the National Mental Health Association, I was able to take three months for writing, thinking, and recharging. In that relatively short time, I did my book on *Values,* explored almost every corner of Ireland, had long overdue quality time with Ann and our youngest, and felt I was on glorious and never-ending holiday. That brief respite will always stand out as a high point of my personal and professional life.

Years later, after two wild years organizing INDEPENDENT SECTOR and the next seven as president, the board provided a

---

Number 15 from a collection of columns entitled "The Voluntary Spirit," by Brian O'Connell. Washington, D.C.: INDEPENDENT SECTOR, 1992. Also adapted from an op-ed piece entitled "Sabbaticals Make For Common Sense," which appeared in *Nonprofit Times* (May 1991).

three-month project leave, which I chose to take over three wonderful Februarys for writing, reflection, and rest.

The enormous significance of those chances to retreat from unrelenting cycles and tigers make me an absolute believer in sabbaticals or project leaves for people who have produced under stress and are expected to do so indefinitely.

Despite how sensible such investments in leaders seem to be, it's not easy to convince nonprofit boards. Recently, a particularly experienced and effective agency head who had been in an absolutely crushing job for fifteen years was turned down for only four months away on grounds she couldn't be spared. Several of us helped to argue for fairness and common sense, and the decision was reversed. That experience made it clear that I have an obligation to put my experience and recommendations in writing to help make the case with other boards that may think they are behaving as good stewards but which, instead, may be using up their most valuable asset.

In response to my request for the related experiences of others, Anne Cohn, executive director of the National Committee for Prevention of Child Abuse, who had received a six-month sabbatical after seven years in the position, wrote: "There are so many reasons why sabbaticals are of value to an institution—more than anything else, perhaps, is the fact they are an important investment in the key personnel of the institution. When leadership is renewed, the organization is renewed."

It is understandable that boards and others worry about coverage during a staff director's absence, but my experience has been that these situations provide other staff members with leadership opportunities that build their capacity and enthusiasm. Even in small organizations, a board member or retired executive from another organization can fill in, which is better than losing the executive altogether.

I've been up against enough reluctant boards to realize that perceptions of sabbaticals make it better to use a different phrase. For that reason, I find myself more often using the term "project leave," though all the time stressing the principle of renewal. The Christian College Coalition describes it thusly: "The purpose for the granting of a sabbatical leave is for study, research, writing, or activities that will contribute significantly to the on-going professional growth and accomplishment of the individual."

In colleges where the practice of sabbaticals is routine, people are generally provided six months off with full pay or a year at half pay after seven years at the job. I encourage voluntary boards to provide three or four months with full pay and benefits. If it's a matter of something or nothing, I urge organizations to start with three months after ten years.

The policy covering sabbaticals or project leaves should apply to all senior and seasoned staff. It's hard to know where a distinct line should be drawn, but it should relate to fairness for past efforts and investment in future participation and effectiveness.

Funders can play a role by setting the pace with their own staff and by providing support for project leaves with grantees to help them bridge the gap. The Chicago Community Trust helps others with its Community Service Fellowships, which each year provide up to $75,000 to three individuals and their agencies to make possible "a growth opportunity . . . for three to fifteen months."

For years, the Carnegie Corporation provided travel leaves for particularly effective and seasoned college presidents. I recall that the president of my alma mater received one of these and found both the recognition and the combination of travel and time away to be absolutely wonderful.

The Durfee Foundation has recently adopted what they call "Avocational Adventure Grants," which allow "carefully selected individuals to have a period of unencumbered time to pursue avocational interests. . . . The purpose is to enhance the lives of creative individuals and as a consequence increase their effectiveness as organization leaders."

There are many different ways an organization can provide for renewal and growth. The Kresge Foundation sometimes trades a staff person with other funders so that both the people and organizations benefit from different perspectives. They also grant flex time for "Release Time Projects." The Christian Medical College Board considers "job related study leaves of two weeks per year"; the Ford Foundation provides project support for heads of orchestras, dance groups and opera companies, and other arts leaders; the Northwest Area Foundation has an

"Educational Leave" policy for special courses, conferences, and other experiences; the Maurice Falk Medical Fund has provided its president with opportunities to be a visiting scholar for teaching and study; and INDEPENDENT SECTOR provides extra time for people to finish books.

There are many ways to achieve what Camus described this way:

> To understand one's world, one must sometimes turn away from it! To serve better, one must briefly hold it at a distance. Where can the necessary solitude be found, the long breathing space in which the mind gathers its strength and takes stock of its courage.

Obviously, I hope that the awarding of opportunities for renewal becomes a wave of the future for philanthropic and voluntary organizations. It will be a sign of our maturity when we recognize that fulfillment of trusteeship includes just such investment in the future of our institutions.

21
Future Leadership in America

INCREASINGLY, WE HEAR the concern expressed that few, if any, leaders are emerging to lead us back to greatness.

In contrast, I submit:

1. that citizen participation and influence are far more significant today than at any time in our history;
2. that the composite leadership in our governmental, business, and voluntary institutions represents the greatest array of leadership in the public interest this country has ever known; and
3. that our interpretation of past greatness is skewed by glasses that are even more magnified than tinted.

Excerpts from the keynote address for the NOW Legal Defense and Education Fund's Tenth Anniversary Convocation, New York City, March 30, 1981.

In terms of citizen participation and influence, a greater proportion of Americans are involved today than at any time in our history. Americans are organizing to influence every conceivable aspect of the human condition. Increasingly, we are willing to stand up and be counted on almost any public issue.

It is important to our national morale, and it is essential to our perspective as we examine such critical issues as "new leadership in the public interest," that we recognize and rejoice in the fact that people still care and still have enormous influence on their lives, their communities, their country, and their world.

It is just as important to realize that this active participation and leadership now reflect every segment of our society. What had largely been the province of the upper classes and then of the upper and middle classes has finally broadened to include all of us. We owe a tremendous debt to the community fathers who served so many causes; but the grandest hurrahs should be reserved for the here-and-now, when participatory democracy has truly come alive with all parts of the population joining in the traditions of service and reform.

I submit that our dilemma is not a dearth of leadership generally, but a natural delay in developing national leaders capable of understanding and capitalizing on the staggering multiplication of participants and the dizzying dispersion of power.

At one extreme, we have many well-meaning people who are so bewildered by the explosion of the power structure into every corner of the community and country that, in order to solve problems, they somehow want to get that power structure back into a manageable system where a smaller group is again in charge.

At the other extreme are those who believe that the lessons of the sixties and seventies have taught us how essential it is that people have greater control of their own destinies. Whether it's expressed as doing one's own thing or empowerment, we are all now rigidly alert to the value and joy of having options and alternatives, and of having the power of citizens to experiment, to influence, and, where necessary, to reform.

In essence, we have been painfully re-learning the fundamental lessons of our ancestors, that independence—of persons and of societies—is the preeminent value.

That lesson has come so hard for many of us that we are suspicious and wary of any interconnections that in any way might detract from our independence. Along the way, we have become skeptical, bordering on cynical, about most of our institutions, even those created to serve or unite us. We want a religious experience but are cool toward organized religion. We want democratic government to serve the common need but are frightened and critical of the bigness of it. We want philanthropy for the support of our causes, but we don't want any self-appointed groups to define the public good. We are aware how many of our aspirations and problems require joint action, but we are not comfortable with the existing vehicles of cooperation.

What has happened is that our attention to independence has vastly outdistanced our attention to the interdependence so necessary to almost everything we want to accomplish.

I suggest that we have now come to the absolutely essential next stage, which involves building a capacity for interdependence that will enhance, not stifle, our uniqueness as individuals and as a society; and I believe that job is the role of the new leadership.

A young California legislator, John Vasconcellos, has contributed to my understanding of the chaos of our times by describing it as a period of "human revolution." In Vasconcellos's terms, this revolution involves a change in our basic assumptions and a challenge to many of our basic institutions. He says that the encouragement is "not that institutions are breaking down, but that people are growing up."

The urgent challenge faced by all of us who are trying to find solutions to staggering public problems is to build or rebuild institutions capable of representing the interdependence of so many diverse people and causes.

There are those who feel that the only way to proceed is to carry the revolution to its ultimate extreme and absolutely level all of our existing social institutions, then rebuild everything from a more democratic base. They are matched and confronted by people and institutions that already have power and who want to hunker down until this unpleasant phase of activism burns out.

If people and organizations concentrate on the things that divide them, or won't participate because the model or the vehicle isn't perfect, then we'll never get anywhere with the complex problems that beset us. It's so easy to tear down and so hard to build, and the world and our institutions are imperfect, but we have to get behind the groups that are building and we have to begin to pull even more than we shove.

The job clearly is not to level the institutions or to quiet the independent voices. The long, complex job facing the new leadership is to build an awareness of our interdependence and to build the vehicles for strengthening it without ignoring or neglecting the yearning and determination of people to be free.

Harlan Cleveland, speaking at the tenth anniversary of Common Cause, commented that "for the past twenty years, people have been ahead of their leaders." He then cited the environment, ecology, civil rights, women's issues, and the Vietnam War as examples.

Michael Walzer, in his recent book *Radical Principles,* enumerates many of the major events of the past twenty years; but as summarized by *Washington Post* reviewer Nick Kotz, "His primary encouragement is the progress toward a democracy of free men and women dedicated both to protecting their individual freedoms and to preserving common purposes."

My point here is to argue that the new leaders are already with us. They are maturing and rising rapidly through the ranks. The three critical stages they are passing through are these:

1. selection for leadership roles by their own groups;
2. the growing ability to recognize and achieve the degree of collaboration usually necessary to the successful pursuit of the goals of most of our organizations;
3. selection and the ability to deal with other, even larger, issues as well as with broader community interests.

The number of men and women passing these tests is wonderfully encouraging. For proof of that, read David Broder's

Changing of the Guard, or read the bios of the representatives and senators elected in 1978 and 1980. Or better, visit almost any city or large rural county and talk to the women and men who serve on the school boards, the health planning agencies, or other voluntary and official groups.

The growth experience of the past two decades needs to mature in the next two, producing national leaders with these four characteristics:

1. a passionate belief in participatory democracy, including the multiplication of participants and the dispersion of power;
2. a capacity to enlarge and to survive the democratic cacophony in order to have a chance to hear the individual shrieks—and songs;
3. an ability to educate the public, including we single-issue players, so that we are better informed of the relationships between our special interests and the larger society in which those interests must be pursued;
4. an ability to make decisions, and to say no— sometimes perhaps even to me and once in a while, maybe even to you.

We are, we must recognize, a nation of leaders demanding to be led and ready to pummel anybody who presumes to come forward.

Let me summarize. We need to be much more aware and encouraged by how many leaders there already are, and by how much caring and service are abroad in this land.

We need to look much less to charismatic leaders to save us and more to the abundant talent already within our ranks.

Once these leaders step forward, voluntarily or otherwise, we need to be at least as fair, objective, and supportive as we demand of them.

The new leaders are already moving into place. Given half a chance, they will serve well the public interest. Many of you in this room represent that new leadership. For most of us, our leadership role is to help clear the way. *You're* coming through, and we are heartened. You, too, take heart. The road is still bumpy, but hang in there—you're on the right track.

22
Independence and Interdependence

THERE'S SO MUCH to be welcomed and admired in all the new self-help guides and such a need to pull away from past patterns of external domination and intimidation that I hesitate to express a caution, or at least a worry, about the pervasive movement towards greater awareness and empowerment of self. It's wonderfully healthy that so many people are struggling to get some control of their own destinies or to find their own personal way. The incisive novelist C.P. Snow observed that a hard core of self-interest is necessary to survival and growth.

As I'll elaborate later, I'm a fierce defender of my own independence and of the need for everyone to be able to get free of the crowd. My worry then is not with the search for independence and self-expression but with the me-first emphasis and tone of so much of the movement. My own experience

From Chapter 7 of *Finding Values That Work: The Search for Fulfillment,* by Brian O'Connell. New York: Walker and Co., 1978.

and everything I see from the Mental Health Association vantage point tells me that independence and interdependence go hand in hand, and that the test of coping and growing is not to let each person fend for him or herself, but for each person to contribute to the balance. If *caring* isn't in the equation, the coping and growing don't hold up.

In a recent *New York Times* review of assorted self-help books, Leonard Levin offered this conclusion:

> But I wonder if it might not be possible to write a successful self-help book that occasionally puts forward—between endless paragraphs of encouragement, approbation, and exculpation—the notion that the reader might have some degree of responsibility for his own behavior and its own consequences for others.

Clearly, and hopefully, we are seeking ways to find ourselves and to exercise our right to march to our different drummers—"however measured or faraway." But at the same time, we can't escape the reality that we are also *all in this together*. Maybe we view our world as a mess, and perhaps the coldness of our surroundings seems to justify alienation and hostility, but more "me-firsters" can only make it a hell of a lot worse. Perhaps we've concluded that it *is* only going to get worse and that we had better get our share while we can, but that has to be the ultimate self-fulfilling prophecy. I'd rather assume that the world is going to last a while and, therefore, try to figure out how we can *all* have it a little better. Not only do I believe that's the way we have to go—if only to keep from going down—but that's the true direction of self-fulfillment.

Dr. Bertram Brown, longtime director of the National Institute of Mental Health, summed up the mutuality of self and service this way:

> I've given a great deal of thought to the pursuit of happiness and have come to the conclusion that it cannot be found except indirectly. The important part of that phrase, "the pursuit of happiness," is the pursuit, the searching and the seeking for something else. If a person substitutes the pursuit of some social goal that serves others

indirectly, then he or she might find happiness and perhaps mental health.

The same thought was expressed in the extreme by Cesar Chavez, as reported by Dr. Robert Coles. Chavez had just concluded an agonizing fast and was participating in a Mass of Thanksgiving, when he delivered this observation on the ultimate meaning of life:

> When we are really honest with ourselves, we must admit that our lives are all that really belong to us. So it is how we use our lives that determines what kind of men we are. It is my deepest belief that only by giving our lives do we find life. I am convinced that the truest act of courage, the strongest act of manliness, is to sacrifice ourselves for others in a totally non-violent struggle for justice. To be a man is to suffer for others. God help us to be men.

Few of us will be called upon to make the ultimate sacrifice, or even really be pressed to demonstrate our humanity, but in a way that gives us an excuse to ignore the smaller ways we can enrich our own lives by helping others. Samuel Johnson said that "He who waits to do a great deal of good at once will probably not do any good."

A past national president of the Mental Health Association, Irving Chase of Boston, was talking to a group in Ohio about the fact that there would never be enough mental health professionals to assist all of us with our search for mental health. He pointed out that of all those who might benefit from mental health services, only seven percent were actually receiving such help. He likened the millions and millions of people who are depressed, desperately lonely, alienated, afraid, or at least grossly unfulfilled to the tip of the iceberg. Afterwards, a man who identified himself as a recently hospitalized patient approached Mr. Chase and said, "I submit that the way we deal with the bottom of the iceberg is to *warm the waters.*"

That phrase and the concept of "warming the waters," offered by a person who clearly knew the searing pain of rejection, is one of those utterly simple, utterly beautiful ideas. It serves better than any philosophy to strip away lesser considerations and to leave us with the obvious fact that it's our daily contribution of warmth and caring that will help us all muddle through. Most of us are always seeking the great moment when the grand design of life will be revealed to us. In the meantime, we rationalize our inactivity on the basis that the clear signal has not yet been received. The truth, of course, is that the grand design unfolds through our composite daily behavior.

I'm a terribly private individual, deeply aware of my own needs for quiet personal time and the freedom to find my own way, but if all that time for self-examination has taught me anything, it's that to be a whole individual I have to be both independent and interdependent, and that my independence won't be worth very much if I don't contribute to the whole.

Erich Fromm argues in his book *Escape From Freedom* that individuals and societies can't, in fact, tolerate total freedom. He says that people find such identity and comfort in being part of tightly structured systems that the constant danger is that we will grow comfortable with authoritarianism. In an otherwise pessimistic view of our future, he concludes that democracy could be the alternative, but only if it is decentralized to the point that people really feel they are, in fact, part of the system. He closes with this glimmer of hope:

> The victory over all kinds of authoritarian systems will be possible only if democracy does not retreat but takes the offensive and proceeds to realize what has been its aim in the minds of those who fought for freedom throughout the last centuries. It will triumph over the forces of nihilism only if it can imbue people with a faith that is the strongest the human mind is capable of, the faith in life and truth, and in freedom as the active and spontaneous realization of the individual self.

There are no shortcuts to happiness, but the most direct route follows the line of service rather than selfishness. The individual who would be fulfilled will sooner or later learn the equation of self and service. The successful searchers will also have learned that happiness isn't found, it's created. The closest I can come to a prescription is equal dosages of independence and interdependence—and plenty of warmth to both core and community. There's no pretension that this formula will necessarily provide blissful contentment. It follows more the course outlined by Aristotle: "Happiness is the utilization of one's talents along lines of excellence." That's the truer direction of fulfillment, and if all that effort and service sometimes cause you to wonder if there isn't an easier way, recall Dag Hammarskjöld's statement that "In our era the road to holiness necessarily passes through the world of action."

Like it or not, we are a terribly interdependent society, and to the extent we each contribute our share to make democracy really work and to "warming the waters," there will be room for individualism, a future for independence, and, as a bonus, this will be a pretty nice place to live together.

23
Investing in Leadership: A Commentary on Applying Common Sense and Proven Models to Resource Development in Nonprofit Organizations

AT A TIME WHEN many leaders of voluntary organizations criticize their counterparts in business for being so fixated on "quarterly results" that they can't see the future, we overlook the fact that our own long-term scopes seem rusted on "today." The nonprofit sector is the most labor intensive of the three sectors but invests by far the least in its future, and it recoils from spending more for fear of being criticized for high overhead. We

---

Unpublished commentary, 1989.

worry about the effectiveness of our organizations, agree on the need to attract more bright young people, shudder at the implications of high staff turnover, talk endlessly about expanding the base of financial and volunteer support, and cringe at the paltry levels of investment and sophistication available for planning and evaluation, but we turn our backs on all this common sense with the rationalization that we are too busy doing good and that no one will give us money to invest in these extras anyway.

At a recent meeting involving the metropolitan heads of one of the country's largest social service organizations, I talked about the alarming mismatch between what they expect of their staffs and what they invest in staff in terms of nominal preparation and development. To a person they agreed, but when I took it the next step and talked about investment in such basics as traineeships, study leaves, and job rotation, the conversation went sour. They scolded that I should know better that they don't have funds for such extras, particularly at a time of serious financial constraints. Before the conversation went stone cold, we calculated that the proportion of their million-dollar budgets that went for staff development was about one percent. My guess is that for the sector as the whole it's even less than that.

When I try to talk about how much businesses spend on Human Resource Development (HRD) and Research and Development (R&D), leaders of voluntary organizations turn me off as though the comparisons were specious. I generate some attention when I indicate how much money even small and medium-sized community governments spend on finding and nurturing young leaders, but the curiosity is mostly grounded in envy. Even volunteer leaders who come from business will only stay with me through the part of the conversation that relates to applying their investment practices, but their interest founders against immediate financial and service deficits.

That contradiction among business leaders applies also to corporate philanthropy, which usually fails to practice what corporations do best. One of the pitfalls many companies fall into involves a natural tendency to model their philanthropy after private foundations, especially the emphasis on program support and the de-emphasis or prohibition against support for financial and organizational development. I keep urging corporate leaders to ask, "What is it that we and the corporation know and do well routinely that, if applied to voluntary organizations and the nonprofit sector generally, might produce the greatest results?" I don't think corporations should emphasize the funding of programs as much as foundations do, but instead should give priority to strengthening the organizations that deal with causes they care about so that these groups can do a better job in the future. INDEPENDENT SECTOR emphasizes the investment idea for philanthropy in general. For example, in our "Blueprint for Substantial Growth in Giving and Volunteering in America," we set forth as an objective: "To help foundations and corporations recognize that investment in the ability of voluntary organizations to attract and develop good management, to raise money, and to involve volunteers is more important for long-term program impact than specific program or project grants." And we add: "Grantmakers should invest in activities designed to strengthen career leadership of nonprofit organizations." My hope is that business leaders especially will practice what they know best when they decide on priorities for their company's giving as well as when they sit as board members of voluntary groups.

Several years ago the Council of Jewish Federations (CJF) undertook an interesting study to try to determine why certain of their local units did so much better than the average. They assumed that the explanation would relate to the number of Jews in those communities, their per-capita income, and the number of Jewish-owned businesses. However, the largest factor by far turned out to be quality of staff as measured by its capacity to effectively involve and provide assistance to an increasing number of volunteer leaders. As a result of that study, the CJF reoriented its national operations to emphasize staff development, including the establishment of the Philip Bernstein Training Center, named after its own able staff director.

Some state and national voluntary organizations try, like businesses, to provide a complete system of courses so that an individual will have an opportunity to be formally trained for the skills required. This begins with a delineation of the needed skills, an appraisal (usually done by somebody higher up in the organization) of the upgrading necessary to achieve those skills, and a planned schedule of courses. These programs usually involve courses run by the parent organization, supplemented by local orientation and refresher courses. They are, of course, dependent on an effective process of supervision, including goal setting and evaluation.

Some organizations, through budget stringencies or enlightened new approaches, have undertaken self-development plans. These, too, begin with an appraisal of performance standards and tasks, but then lead into greater self-appraisal of areas where improvement is needed as well as self-direction in seeking assistance to develop the necessary skills. Individuals involved in such a program are usually assisted by a staff development specialist in their self-assessment as well as in the development of their learning plans.

Many agencies are combining these two models. This approach stems from budget limitations and an awareness that if individuals are to grow, they must be intimately involved in shaping their own development.

Several years ago I was involved in a project designed to meet some emergency training needs. The California Heart Association, which I headed, was at a stage where it was developing far more rapidly than we could realistically handle. We faced a tremendous need to quickly develop new staff skills. We worked with local staff members throughout the state in identifying the skills they felt most in need of. Then we worked together to develop a profile that identified the skills the person's job required and arrived at a mutual determination of which of those skills most needed developing. We then identified the formal courses that were available within our national office, the American Heart Association, and, where appropriate, targeted people for these.

We developed certain other courses which we were trained to conduct. Other courses needed to be developed on an interagency basis, and we developed these in conjunction with the California Lung Association, the Society for Crippled Children and Adults, and the Cancer Society. Lastly, we identified the relevant continuing education courses offered by educational institutions within California. Through this process we were able to identify or develop the resources to deal with most of the skills needed and to project a training schedule for each professional staff member.

During that same California crisis we also developed a trainee program that attracted to the association younger people who wanted a career in public service. Because the first jobs into which we placed trainees required that they have work experience, we did not try to hire students right out of college or graduate school for the program. Instead, we turned to persons who had been involved in other activities for one to five years and were looking for a change. We provided one month of training in the state office, four months of placement in a local chapter, and a final one-month wrap-up again at the state office. Most of these people were quickly moved into jobs throughout the state and have since developed into significant staff leaders within the Heart Association and other agencies.

In a recent three-year study that INDEPENDENT SECTOR conducted to determine what factors are most likely to lead to organizational effectiveness in voluntary institutions, the single most important factor turned out to be "the presence of an individual, usually the staff director, who truly leads the organization and creates a culture that enables and motivates the organization to fulfill its mission." It's my own experience after thirty-five years as a community organizer that associations and the sector as a whole rarely devote much real attention to understanding the characteristics of good staff leaders; to the early recruitment of them from colleges and universities; to involvement in traineeships and job development; or to other common sense aspects involving the cultivation of future leaders.

A sequel to the CJF experience illustrates one way we can begin to attend to long-term investment. During the federation's study, one of the leaders was Morton Mandel, chairman and CEO of Premier Industrial Corporation. When both his corporation and family foundation were planning to expand their philanthropy, I was among those consulted about what new areas they might emphasize. I reminded them of the CJF experience and told them of my notion that businesspeople should apply HRD and R&D to their philanthropy. In addition, I indicated that a family with their widespread community and, indeed, national and international charitable interests should try to figure out what they could do that might advance many of their causes. I added that I thought we had to get as basic as tapping the pool of public service–minded young people in colleges and universities and build bridges for many of them into jobs and future leadership roles with philanthropic and voluntary organizations. Mr. Mandel later indicated that those early conversations led to the establishment of what is now the Mandel Center for Nonprofit Organizations at Case Western University. The center provides and promotes undergraduate attention to the responsibilities of citizenship; offers graduate courses and degrees relating to nonprofit organizations; conducts and stimulates research, with an emphasis on leadership and management of voluntary institutions; and provides training for volunteer and staff leaders.

The Bernstein Training Center of the CJF and the Mandel Center at Case Western are encouraging new examples of investing in a specific organization and the sector as a whole.

Yale University was the first to establish a center devoted to nonprofit studies. Their Program on Nonprofit Organizations was established in 1977. Since then at least eighteen additional centers have been established to focus on research, education, and training. Indiana's University Center on Philanthropy, which like Mandel is comprehensive, even includes a unit called the Fundraising School that is devoted to providing training to volunteer and staff leaders who have responsibility for financial development in churches, hospitals, museums, schools, and the full range of nonprofit organizations. The Institute for Nonprofit Organization Management at the University of San Francisco focuses primarily on training mid-career managers but also sponsors important efforts in research and conferencing. The Lincoln Filene Center at Tufts University is quite comprehensive and includes a major training program for trustees of voluntary and public boards such as school and community mental health boards.

Beyond the centers themselves, there are now more than a hundred colleges that offer individual courses on philanthropy and voluntary activity. At least as many institutions also provide organized programs to encourage students to become involved in community service. These efforts are assisted by the Campus Compact and administered by the Education Commission of the States and by the Campus Outreach Opportunity League

(COOL), which is organized and run by students and recent graduates. Another group founded by students and still influenced largely by them is ACCESS, which attempts to provide information and assistance to students about job possibilities in voluntary organizations.

There is growing recognition that higher education in general should return to the prominent role it embraced and fulfilled a century ago by helping prepare young people for public responsibility. In 1985 I was asked to keynote the annual meeting of the American Association of Higher Education on the topic "Citizenship and Community Service: Are They a Concern and Responsibility of Higher Education?" I said, in part, that it was "absolutely clear to me that 1) educated persons in our society should have a far better grasp of how this country does its public business; 2) they should be conditioned for the lifetime obligations and rewards of community service; and 3) the education system at all levels has a critical responsibility for that result."

. . . .

Nurturing civic responsibility and voluntary organizations is by no means a sole responsibility of academic centers and institutions. Many other centers, such as the National Executive Service Corp, Support Centers of America, and many of the local Technical Assistance Centers (TACs), have been at this job a long time.

All of these efforts depend upon a growing body of literature. From the start, INDEPENDENT SECTOR's Research Committee recognized that we could not build and sustain significant research and education efforts without a much larger literature. Fortunately, several publishers, including the Foundation Center, Jossey-Bass, Greenwood Press/Praeger Books, DC Heath, Indiana University Press, Lexington Books, MacMillan, Oxford University Press, Sage Publications, the Taft Group, and Transaction Books, are beginning to address this need. Ten years ago, John Gardner indicated that there were whole libraries devoted to both business and public administration, but that "you could put into a Boy Scout's backpack all of the basic books about the independent sector." At that time, we were lucky to see a book a year. Now, by recent count, there is a new one approximately every two weeks.

There is also a growing research establishment beyond the centers and other programs mentioned above. Since the early 1980s, INDEPENDENT SECTOR has been publishing an annual "Research in Progress," which lists research activity known to us. Current listings are about seven times what they were just a few years ago. IS, with the assistance of the United Way Institute, conducts an annual Research Forum that is also growing remarkably in the number of participants and quality of research reported.

There is rapid growth in the development of publications and training opportunities for specific categories of volunteers and staff. Among these is the national Center for Nonprofit Boards, which was established jointly by the Association of Governing Boards of Universities and Colleges and INDEPENDENT SECTOR. Other training activities focus on accounting, legal issues, fundraising, planning, executive searches, and much more.

. . . .

Certainly one can't dismiss the importance of realistic salary scales and fringe benefits. These must be a part of the effort to attract, promote, and hold good people. Various surveys indicate that salaries run one-third to one-half those in comparable jobs in government and industry. In an important study, "Work and Work Force Characteristics in the Nonprofit Sector," Philip Mirvis and Edward Hackett reported that "nonprofit jobs provide more challenge, variety, satisfaction and intrinsic rewards than those in private enterprise or government." Their findings indicate that these satisfactions will attract and help retain people as long as the salary differential is no more than one-third of what they could make in other sectors.

To achieve the full benefits of some of these investment efforts the sector is going to have to learn to work much more cooperatively. For example, it's not realistic to expect many voluntary organizations, even large ones, to set up recruitment programs at a significant number of universities. There will need to be some vehicle developed for pooled and cooperative efforts. That will also apply to certain kinds of traineeships and career ladders. For many organizations, there will also be a need for joint fringe benefit programs such as those provided by TIAA for educational and research groups and Mutual of America for health and social welfare organizations. Even broader cooperative efforts, such as reaching out to public administration, will be necessary to broaden the concept of careers in public service.

For an annual meeting of the New York Regional Association of Grantmakers, I was asked to address the question "Is there a Career in Grantmaking?" I had to answer no, but I followed up by stating, "I hope we can achieve the concept of a career within the sector, or at least within the area of public service generally." I then went on to list several steps that I thought would contribute to reaching that point and concluded by saying, "The only way we can get from here to there is to start with an awareness that the essential ingredient of effectiveness and excellence in philanthropic and voluntary organizations is the quality of the people involved. It will also take an awareness that the career is probably in the sector generally . . . and, consistent with my constant message to grantmakers, that we will need a greater willingness by grantmakers to invest in building the capacity of the sector, with an emphasis on people. While the lessons of the search for excellence belong with all of us, some real part of the opportunity for change must involve the grantmakers who are in the best position to invest in the capacity of this sector to be of even greater public service, which is after all our ultimate standard of excellence."

I suggest that even enlightened funders who are inclined to support organizational development won't take an interest in an organization that doesn't demonstrate confidence and investment in its own future. Investing in leadership begins at home.

24

The Growth Fund

TO: _____ Corporation

FROM: Brian O'Connell

DATE: January 2, 1991

SUBJECT: Rationale for Corporations to Apply to Nonprofit Organizations the Lessons That Successful Businesses Apply to Their Own Effectiveness and Growth

As you requested, I am putting in writing some of the ideas we discussed about making an even greater impact with your company's already significant philanthropic program.

These communications, relating to greater corporate investment in the effectiveness and growth of the independent sector, were requested by one of the country's largest corporate funders after discussions about ways to strengthen its philanthropic impact. The company's subsequent financial decline and change of leadership sidetracked implementation.

As I indicated, a surprising limitation of corporate philanthropy is that it does not emphasize what businesses know and do best. It doesn't concentrate on applying to nonprofit organizations the experience and lessons of successful businesses that contribute to effectiveness and growth. Corporations model private foundations in supporting *program* initiatives rather than development initiatives that could build the capacity of nonprofit organizations to sustain and expand program efforts.

Business executives, including contributions officers, routinely decry the failure of nonprofit organizations to deal with such basic issues as providing adequate salaries and benefits to attract and hold good staff; engage in common sense planning; apply research and marketing techniques to program development; or invest realistically in long-term financial development. But it is the rare corporation that links basic business practices to its grantmaking. Corporate public-service officers are every bit as disdainful as foundation officers when someone dares to suggest that they should consider fundraising. Somehow, corporations that measure success in annual sales and profits, *and* which criticize nonprofits for not being more businesslike, find it offensive or at least inappropriate to focus their assistance on effectiveness and growth.

When Eugene Dorsey moved from the business side of Gannett to head the Gannett Foundation, he was shocked and discouraged when I told him that corporate philanthropy represented only 5 percent of all giving in the United States. He wondered whether 5 percent could really make that much difference until he figured out that if the 5 percent was viewed as an engine to build an even better and larger 95 percent, then corporate philanthropy could make a large difference.

If your corporation, with its reputation for both business success and public service, were to turn more of its attention and leverage to the effectiveness and growth of voluntary organizations, it would enable the nonprofit sector to expand its service far beyond what more program project support will buy.

The following is a sketch of the kinds of investment efforts through which the corporation could jolt and assist nonprofit leaders to begin to fulfill their seriously neglected responsibilities relating to effectiveness and growth.

A Program for Nonprofit Effectiveness and Growth

EXAMPLES OF POSSIBLE INITIATIVES

1. Academy for Nonprofit Leaders

Training center(s) for top volunteer and staff leaders, including the team of board chairman and executive director, to be *trained* about such leadership responsibilities as planning, financial development, board development, evaluation, etc. Emphasis would be on training the leaders of national umbrella groups (National Health Council, Opera America, National Council of La Raza, etc.) to learn and develop their continuing roles to provide such training for their affiliates.

The Academy would also be the vehicle for meetings of nonprofit leaders and others to discuss and develop solutions for such impediments to growth as inadequate salaries, board timidity about spending money on investment, inadequate recruitment on campuses, failure of foundations and corporations to fund investment, etc.

Joint meetings of business and nonprofit leaders on applying to nonprofit organizations the lessons of successful businesses that contribute to effectiveness and growth.

This would be the nonprofit sector's Command and General Staff College, where the top leaders would finally have a place to come together to consider the larger issues relating to the sector's role and future and where the leadership's responsibilities to deal with those issues would be emphasized.

2. Traineeships for Careers in Community Service

A program to initiate an ongoing practice by umbrella groups (Council on Foundations, American Heart Association, Catholic Charities, etc.) of having a recruitment and basic training program to attract, orient, train, and place bright young people into jobs in this sector and to assist these people in gaining increased and broadening experience. There should be a central place and placement center where the various programs are coordinated and people are tracked and encouraged.

3. Fellowships

For early and mid-career "comers" and for "people builders."

A dual program to 1) recognize the "people builders" and to highlight the value of mentoring; and 2) to provide "comers" with opportunities for exposure to those mentors.

The mentors or people builders might be the senior fellows, honored and rewarded for their special roles, and the comers might be the junior fellows, who are honored and rewarded by their description as (company) "Fellows" and by exposure to a known and recognized mentor.

During each cycle of the fellowships (6 or 12 months), there would be a meeting of all the current senior and junior (company) Fellows, with separate sessions for the mentors to spark and learn from one another.

4. Studies in Nonprofit Effectiveness and Growth

(Could be part of the Academy.)

Commissioned studies and reports on matters that relate to acceleration of, or impediments to, growth and effectiveness. This is where we could get at such central issues as analyzing and publishing the skills, attributes, and experiences of people who succeed in various key jobs in the sector.

5. Financial Development Grants

A relatively few (15–25?) grants per year, competitively selected for support of the best fund-raising plans in various categories such as size, grassroots, human services, self-help, religion, etc. The process of developing a plan would itself be a valuable experience for board and staff, and the experiences of the winners would be tracked and publicized to spread the lessons.

Far beyond the process and examples, the initiative would spread the word that (the company) recognizes financial development as a primary responsibility of good leadership and management.

6. Staff Development Grants

Somewhat like the financial development grants to support a selected number of superior plans by organizations in various categories that will help us all learn how to break the salary impediments, create pooling of funds for adequate benefit plans, develop a study leave plan for long-term staff in danger of burnout, establish job-trading experiences for 6 to 12 months, experiment with executive director preparation training, etc.

Though it's probably obvious and is indicated elsewhere, it's worth repeating that though such activities would be *very* important of themselves, the larger contribution would be that (the company), with all of its credibility and power, would be moving in to make clear that the field can no longer tolerate the failure to face up to leadership responsibilities relating to effectiveness and growth, and that funders have to begin to pay at least as much attention to institution building as they do to program support for organizations in which they have confidence and in which they and the rest of us will depend for growing service and impact.

SECOND MEMO

October 3, 1992

In response to our further discussions and your request, I'm providing a more specific plan relating to the corporation's investment in the effectiveness and growth of the independent sector.

The Growth Fund
A _____ Company Investment Initiative for Nonprofit Enterprise

The Growth Fund is a project to apply to nonprofit endeavor the capacity building strategies practiced routinely by successful businesses.

The project has four parts:

> 1. To build into the sector's orientation and practice the idea that investment in capacity building is an essential and seriously neglected responsibility of philanthropic and voluntary organizations.
>
> 2. To assist the sector in identifying significant impediments to growth within the sector, such as inadequate recruitment and retention of able staff, and to apply strategies for dealing with those impediments.
>
> 3. To provide matching funds to support competitively selected projects, from a variety of voluntary organizations, that have the greatest likelihood of demonstrating that investment in growth pays off.
>
> 4. To publicize examples of investment activities of philanthropic and voluntary organizations that are considered models of capacity building.

By establishing the Growth Fund, the _____ Company would demonstrate that a realistic part of grantmaking, especially by corporations, should be directed to helping nonprofits learn what businesses know and do best, which involves investing in effectiveness and growth.

In a chapter entitled "Investing More Money In Fund-Raising—Wisely," in the recently released *Taking Fund Raising Seriously,* Wilson Levis writes:

> There is general agreement that giving must increase at a faster rate if nonprofits are to provide urgently needed services. However, increasing giving at a faster rate of growth will require wise investment in fund raising at a faster rate. What is the current investment in fund raising? Using an industry estimate of 15 percent average fund-raising costs, the nonprofit sector spent $16 billion in 1988 to raise $104 billion and net $88 billion for programs. Was it worth $16 billion? If nonprofits had not invested $15 billion in fund raising in 1988, tens of millions of people, in fact all of us, would not have benefited from the $88 billion of net funds raised.
>
> What if the sector had invested $25 billion in fund raising? Could it have raised $140 billion and netted $115 billion? Research indicates that there is a vast untapped potential for giving in this country. However, other research into the economics of charitable fund raising indicates that such an increase could not have been accomplished without first investing additional money. The nonprofit sector urgently needs to realize this, set aside its negative attitudes toward fund-raising costs, and start taking the rate of growth of fundraising budgets seriously.

The Growth Fund might exist for five years and involve investments of $1 million a year. Its success would be measured by changes in the attitudes and behavior of the leaders of the philanthropic and voluntary organizations as demonstrated by successfully investing a larger proportion of their budgets to assure maximum impact and growth.

SPECIFIC ACTIVITIES:

1. To build into the sector's organization and practice an awareness that investment in capacity building is an essential and seriously neglected responsibility of philanthropic and voluntary organizations.

1.1 The very establishment of the Growth Fund and the company's role in it will send a shock wave through the sector, waking its leaders to the reality that trusteeship involves building for greater service and impact.

1.2 The company will establish a Leadership Council of top business leaders and volunteer and staff leaders, including health, religion, social welfare, arts, environment, international, etc. to help the sector face up to the legitimacy and sensibleness of capacity building.

1.3 With the help of IS, the company would convene the leadership of existing umbrella groups, perhaps annually during the life of the Growth Fund, to focus on their responsibility for capacity building. These umbrella groups include the full spectrum of the sector, such as the Council of Foundations, the National Health Council, Opera America, the Council of Jewish Federations, the National Assembly of Social Welfare Organizations, and so on.

2. To assist the company, IS would help identify significant impediments to growth within the sector and apply for strategies for dealing with them.

2.1 Documenting the lack of investment in recruiting and nurturing public service–minded young people.

2.2 Creation of pooled efforts for recruitment, traineeships, job placement, training, transfers, etc.

2.3 Attention to the enormous need for adequate starting salaries and salary scales to attract and hold effective people.

2.4 Creation of affordable, available, and portable benefit packages and adequate training of board members to recognize their responsibility to provide such benefits.

2.5 Development of training programs for the teams of top volunteer and top staff leaders, beginning with the major umbrella groups and, through them, their affiliates, members, grantees, etc.

3. To provide matching funds to support competitively selected projects, from a variety of voluntary organizations, that have the greatest likelihood of demonstrating that investment in growth pays off. The grant money would match funds put up by the competing organizations as their own demonstration of investment commitment.

3.1 Support of traineeship for careers in public service. This would be a program to stimulate such efforts as an ongoing practice by the natural umbrella groups so that they would begin to devote attention to regular recruitment and basic training programs to attract, orient, train, and place bright young people into jobs in the sector and to assist these people in gaining broadening experience. There should be a central place where the various programs are coordinated.

3.2 Establishment of fellowships. These would be for early and mid-career "comers" and for "people builders." This would be a dual program to: 1) recognize and encourage "people builders"; and 2) to provide to the "comers" recognition and exposure to the mentors.

The mentors or people builders would be the senior fellows, honored and rewarded for their special roles, and the comers would be the junior fellows who are honored and rewarded by their description as "(Company) Fellows" and by exposure to a known and recognized mentor.

During each cycle of the fellowships, there would be a meeting of all the current senior and junior (Company) Fellows, with separate sessions for the mentors to spark and learn from one another.

3.3 Establishment of financial development grants. These would be relatively few, perhaps 15 to 25 grants per year, competitively selected for support of the best plans in various categories such as size, grassroots, human services, self-help, religion, etc. The process of developing a plan would itself be a valuable experience for board and staff, and the experiences of the winners would be tracked and publicized to spread the lessons.

Far beyond the process and example, the initiative would spread the word that the (company) recognizes financial development as a primary responsibility of good leadership and management.

3.4 Establishment of staff development grants. These would be somewhat like the financial development grants for a selected number of superior plans by competing organizations in various categories, and would help us all learn how to bread the salary impediments, create pooling funds for creative benefit plans, develop a leave study plan for long-term staff in danger of burnout, establish job training experiences, experiment with executive director preparation training, etc.

4. To publicize examples of investment activities of philanthropic and voluntary organizations that are considered models of capacity building.

4.1 Use INDEPENDENT SECTOR's extensive communication network to regularly alert our members and their affiliates, members, and grantees to good investment models.

4.2 To use the experience of INDEPENDENT SECTOR's "Profiles of Excellence" study and publication of its book by that title to create a pamphlet and monograph series.

4.3 Prepare a book on the subject of investment for capacity building.

4.4 Regularly use INDEPENDENT SECTOR's annual meeting and other gatherings to highlight the priority of investment and provide effective examples of it.

4.5 Use the meetings of the natural umbrella groups to do the same.

The second memo ended with suggestions for the company's administration of the program and thoughts about future steps. Though the company was not able to move ahead as planned, perhaps someday another company, foundation, or group of grantmakers will establish something like the Growth Fund.

25

The Future Looks Good—For Those Who Invest in It

My assignment is to identify some of the "big issues" for the next 10 to 25 years that will almost certainly influence the future of voluntary institutions.

I divided my analysis into the following categories: 1) the capacity for giving and volunteering; 2) public attitudes and behavior; 3) the positive trends that can be nurtured; 4) evidences of impact; 5) investment in organizational and financial development; 6) governmental oversight; 7) international implications; and 8) research to understand more accurately our role in society and how to fulfill it. For each of the categories, I've limited myself to five points.

Requested article, 25th anniversary issue of *Fund Raising Management,* March 1994.

From this analysis, I come away all the more optimistic about the future, but only if we invest in fostering the many positive factors while countering some negative ones.

Capacity for Giving and Volunteering

Perhaps the most positive point is that it is wonderfully clear that the wellspring of generosity is deep and far from tapped out.

1. Even in these tough economic times, there are repeated reports of staggering successes in campaigns that reached for hundreds of millions, and even billions, of dollars, and one of the key factors rests with tapping new prospects.
2. INDEPENDENT SECTOR's surveys continue to indicate that the proportion of income contributed by middle- and even low-income givers is greater than that provided by all but the upper categories of the well-to-do.
3. In all categories of income there is a growing proportion of tithers and fivers as well as growing evidence that when people recognize and understand the symbol and standard of Give Five (five percent of income and five hours per week to the causes of their choice), they move toward that leadership rank.
4. Less than 10 percent of the givers with annual incomes over a quarter of a million dollars provide more than 50 percent of all that is given by people at that income level.
5. The largest single reason people give is that they are asked, and the more personal the request the more likely the gift.

Public Attitudes and Behavior

1. Our studies continue to indicate that public confidence in nonprofit organizations is very high.

Obviously, nothing in this observation should cause indifference, but at least the public thinks well of what we do and assumes that we do our work more efficiently than government and with greater concern for individuals than either government or business. It believes that we work toward our goals in an honorable and humane way, with continuing regard for the rights and needs of individuals.

2. The public is forgiving if an organization acknowledges its difficulties and works openly to correct them. Covenant House has already returned to its prior level of support and many United Ways have continued to grow.

3. It should also be viewed as good news rather than bad that in the face of recent transgressions and negative publicity, the public is becoming increasingly discerning. To merit support, organizations have to be seen as more open, accountable, and able to prove their effectiveness. Good performance is by far the best way to fulfill public trust.

4. Individual organizations and the sector as a whole should help the public distinguish between effective and ineffective performance. The public should know what questions to ask, where to get information, how to interpret reports—all those skills which enable people to make more informed decisions about appeals for their time and money.

5. Ninety percent of the American people contribute money and more than 50 percent are active volunteers. People want to be involved. Asking, with a clear case, is still the best way to do it.

Making the Most of the Positive Trends

1. Our recent studies make clear that the baby boomers are becoming generous with their time and money, and that teens are even more inclined to accept

responsibility for service to community. Given the enormous size of these age categories (14 to 44!) and their attitudes about involvement, if we will nurture and build on these favorable attributes the future can be bright indeed.

2. Giving of time and money involves a broadening spectrum of Americans, including more older people, men, low-income families, and people with problems themselves.
3. Among all the categories, the generosity of persons of color is expanding dramatically. Growing diversity throughout the sector is a particular strength.
4. People feel good about being involved and knowing they can make a difference. They admire and envy those who are seen as active volunteers.
5. Organizations that continue to invest in the quality of their asking continue to set the trend for growth.

Evidence of Impact

1. Increasingly, we hear the lament that Americans don't really have a civic spirit any more. There is a pervasive view that in earlier times we were far more willing than we are today to help one another and to become involved in causes and public issues. Actually, the past was not as good as remembered and the present is far better than perceived.
2. A far larger proportion and many more parts of our population are involved in community service today than at any time in our history.
3. Whether one's interest is wildflowers or civil rights, arthritis or clean air, Oriental art or literacy, the dying or the unborn, organizations are already at work, and if they do not suit our passion, it is possible to start our own.
4. We organize to serve every conceivable aspect of the human condition and are willing to stand up and be

counted on almost any public issue. We organize to fight zoning changes, approve bond issues, improve garbage collection, expose overpricing, enforce equal rights, and protest wars.

5. In very recent times we have successfully organized to deal with the rights of women, conservation and preservation, learning disabilities, conflict resolution, Hispanic culture and rights, education on the free enterprise system, the aged, voter registration, the environment, Native Americans, the dying, experimental theater, international understanding, population control, neighborhood empowerment, control of nuclear power, consumerism, and on and on. Our interests and impact extend from neighborhoods to the ozone layer and beyond.

Investment in Organizational and Financial Development

1. Boards are far more alert today to their responsibility for organizational effectiveness, including their own stewardship.
2. More boards are beginning to understand that stewardship does not only mean careful harboring of assets, *but* also effective investment of them to increase an organization's ability to fulfill its mission. More organizations now understand their responsibility to invest in fundraising.
3. Though we are by far the most labor-intensive of the three sectors, there is still very little invested by organizations or the sector as a whole in recruitment, retention, and development of staff.
4. As inadequate as staff development is, there is even less attention paid to systematic recruitment, training, placement, and advancement of volunteers.
5. One of the bright lights is the growth of academic attention to the sector. Perhaps someday we will return to the point where we were a hundred years

ago, when the very definition of an educated person included orientation to and preparation for a lifetime of active citizenship and community service.

Governmental Oversight

1. Next to the possible loss of public confidence, the greatest danger involves governmental encroachments on the independence that is the sector's most important characteristic and contribution. Nothing in this should deny or impede the government's absolutely appropriate responsibility to be certain that voluntary organizations are worthy of the special privileges provided by tax exemption.
2. The full range and intensity of current problems cannot be covered here, but examples include:
    a. the very definition of what an exempt organization is and can do;
    b. a pervasive misunderstanding that exemption is deserved only by organizations that serve the poorest in our society.
    c. revenue shortfalls of all levels of government overriding the need to support and sustain voluntary initiative;
    d. destructive confusion about the relative roles of the three sectors.
3. There are serious incursions on the freedoms of speech, assembly, and association, often taking the form of challenges to the advocacy role of voluntary groups.
4. There are very real questions being raised about whether certain institutions or even whole parts of the sector are still worthy of tax exemption. This is particularly so in health-care institutions, which are being challenged to prove their charitable or public purpose.

5. Though the problems are outstripping our ability to deal with them effectively, at least we are much better organized than we were 10 or 25 years ago, thanks in part to the presence and impact of such groups as NSFRE, state associations of nonprofits, and IS.

International Implications

1. It is instructive how many different governments and economies are struggling to emulate our strong voluntary independent sector.
2. Most of us are realizing that to deal effectively with the missions of our organizations, whether they relate to health, the environment, or human rights, we have to develop global strategies and partnerships.
3. The competition for funds gets more intense as other countries make the case for even more urgent needs.
4. Fund-raising strategies long successful in the United States are often not adequate for appeals beyond the borders.
5. Asking becomes a great deal more complex, even in our appeals to foreign companies operating here in the United States.

Research to Understand More Accurately Our Role in Society and How to Fulfill It

1. There is a fairly urgent need to more clearly understand and articulate the roles *and* the limitations of voluntary organizations. For example, one of the key lessons of the Reagan years was that we make a grave mistake if we exaggerate what voluntary organizations can do, particularly if that allows us to exaggerate what government *need* not do.

2. There is also an urgent need to understand the changing roles and relationships of the three sectors, including the problems of overlap and competition.
3. If we are going to convince the public of our worth, we need to understand and articulate far better than we do at present the impact of philanthropic and voluntary organizations as well as public attitudes about us.
4. Applied research in the development of fundraising effectiveness is obviously the order of the day.
5. Similarly, we have to devote a good deal more research to marketing, planning, evaluation, collaboration, and much more.

Obviously, the news is not all good, but in my view the outlook for the sector is decidedly positive. For the individual organization that has a worthy cause, is open and accountable, and invests in its development, the outlook is very bright.

My summary then is that the future looks good—for those who invest in it.

26

Citizenship and Community Service: Are They a Concern and Responsibility of Higher Education?

THE UNITED STATES is the longest-lived democracy in the history of the world. This democracy has provided almost all of us with greater freedom and opportunity than any nation of human beings has ever known. Among the crucial factors that foster and preserve that democracy and those freedoms are active citizenship and personal community service. There are clear signs, however, that citizen participation and community service may not be as vital a part of our society for the current

---

Excerpts from the keynote address of that title, American Association of Higher Education's National Conference on Higher Education, Chicago, 1985.

younger generations and those who come after them. No leader or leadership institution—particularly no educator or educational institution—can presume that fostering active citizenship to prolong our democracy and to extend those glorious freedoms for those who come after us is someone else's business.

. . . .

I was told that one of the reasons I was asked to do this talk is because I am not part of "the education establishment," and that at this stage you wanted someone who could come at this topic a bit unfettered.

The danger in that approach is that the outsider tends to put in all kinds of disclaimers and qualifications and hesitates to be very definite about anything. Harry Truman is reported to have suggested that the best person to ask for advice or opinion should only have one arm. People like that, he said, are least likely to respond, "Well, on the one hand this, but on the other hand that."

I want to be fairly definite in sharing with you how this outsider sees your responsibility and then leave it to you to determine how much of it fits.

Being unencumbered with your view of the various factors, I can say that it is absolutely clear to me that: (1) educated persons in our society should have a far better grasp of how this country does its public business; (2) that they should be conditioned for the lifetime obligations and rewards of community service; and (3) that the education system at all levels has a critical responsibility to ensure that result.

Without trying to be inclusive, let me indicate five roles for higher education in the development of active citizenship and personal community service.

Research

Subjects so important to our basic freedoms as active citizenship and personal community service should not be considered as soft, peripheral, or unworthy of scholarly pursuit. In the paper "Major Challenges to Philanthropy," Robert Payton, who serves as chairperson of INDEPENDENT SECTOR's Research Committee, writes: "There are few fields of such vast magnitude that have stimulated such little curiosity among scholars."

It is our Research Committee's aim that more scholars, academic disciplines, and institutions will take an active interest in this sector so that it will become a legitimate and attractive field for scholarship. We don't even know much about the origins of this pluralism and participation, and there is little literature describing or attesting to its significance. Even well-educated people usually just guess that it probably stems from the Protestant ethic and only recall de Tocqueville having written much about it.

That is a large part of why I did the book *America's Voluntary Spirit,* to try to spark greater awareness and interest in the origins, dimensions, and impact of our independent sector and to give us all someone other than de Tocqueville to quote. In the introduction to the book, I call attention to the absolutely basic matter of understanding those origins:

> From where does all this generosity stem? Obviously, ours is not the only participatory society in the world. Giving, volunteering and nonprofit organizations exist in many countries, but nowhere else are the numbers, proportions and impact so great. . . .
>
> Why is there so much more of this activity here? It's not easy to sort out, but if we hope to sustain it into future generations, we need to understand the phenomenon better than we do. The research and literature are sparse.

I submit that the issues of active citizenship and voluntary association should become a part of the agenda, including the valid tenure track for scholars in history, religion, government, philosophy, economics, psychology, sociology, arts, law, and virtually every other discipline.

Research on this topic is academically legitimate and absolutely essential if we are to have a firm grasp of the roots and persistence of our liberty.

Teaching

For all the same reasons, the matters of citizenship and community service are important to teach.

The educated person must understand (1) the relationship between citizenship and freedom; and (2) the relationship between the rights of citizens to organize themselves and the freedom of citizens.

We have never found a better substitute for safeguarding freedom than placing responsibility in the hands of the people and expecting them to fulfill it. We can be disappointed at times in their performance, but the ultimate answer is still the democratic compact, recently beautifully and bluntly restated by John Gardner:

> "Freedom and responsibility,
> Liberty and duty—
> That's the deal."

Career Development for Public Service

Without getting into the middle of your marathon debate about education versus training, it is obvious that higher education does educate a great many people for a number of professions and specialties, including specific areas of public service such as public health, public administration, and teaching.

There is an immediate and urgent need to be certain that in all such fields, people are given a far better understanding of how this country does its public business. For example, in my own area of public administration, most graduates are trained only for their important roles in civil service and come out with little or no grasp of such basics as citizenship education, the role of philanthropy and voluntary organizations in influencing public policy, or the role of voluntary organizations in carrying out public services. I went to the Maxwell School, which even has in its name the word *citizenship*, but by the time I got there the focus related almost entirely to the internal workings of government and pretty much ignored the broader elements of citizenship.

Thus, even in the one area of professional development where it would seem to be most obvious that people should come away with a grasp of how this country operates, the matters of citizenship and community service are pretty much overlooked.

Beyond the existing career tracks, we need to develop more specific ways by which young people are given exposure and learning opportunities relating to public service, including jobs in philanthropic and voluntary organizations. Many young people today are interested in public service, but they have little grasp of what the opportunities are and little training for them. I know of no part of our society so central to our well-being and so dependent on human resources in which so little attention is given to people development.

Attention to Older Students Who Are Volunteer or Staff Leaders of Nonprofit Organizations

Institutions of higher education have an enormous opportunity and obligation to help citizens understand the larger framework in which they work, as well as to prepare them for their tasks as volunteer and staff leaders.

Recognizing that most people do not receive much grounding in the basics of citizenship and community service, and are not likely to for many years to come, colleges and universities can perform a large service by providing older students with courses that give grounding in such basics as the relative roles and powers of mayors, city councils, and school boards; the relative roles of city, county, and state government; the relative roles of the three sectors; alternative service delivery systems; public financing; and so on. More specifically, these institutions can provide staff with needed training in marketing, planning, program evaluation, fundraising, and so on.

There is a need and a hunger for assistance on the part of citizens who serve as board members as well as in other volunteer capacities. There is general acknowledgment of the important role of citizen boards for both governmental and nonprofit organizations but extraordinarily little attention paid to helping citizens fulfill these roles. I have just completed a two-year project on board development that will include the publication next month of *The Board Member's Book.* In the course of my efforts to identify good resource materials I realized that the important topic of board development has not achieved sufficient status to have generated its own body of literature.

There is just about no place where a conscientious volunteer can turn for guidance on the effectiveness of boards and the role of board members in planning, evaluation, fundraising, and other essential board functions. The topic, indeed the whole subject of the independent sector, can be characterized as in a "pamphleteering" stage, or, in the jargon of librarians, as "fugitive" or "ephemeral" material. The literature is still a long way from giving the sector the intellectual underpinnings it deserves.

Even institutions that make a great deal of their income by attracting older students and which try to respond to the needs of their communities seem rarely to provide courses that relate to the responsibilities of the thousands of local persons who serve on the boards of churches and synagogues, museums and other cultural organizations, hospitals and health agencies, and all the other kinds of nonprofit organizations that depend on citizen leadership.

Citizenship Education

I am often involved in consultation with foundations that are trying to figure out how they can have greater influence on the major issues of the day. Very frequently, after I have outlined some of the issues, such as making our cities work, improving public education systems, ending racism, conquering cancer, or controlling nuclear arms, I get the response that those issues are beyond the foundation's role, resources, and ability to influence. My reply is always that if these are the major issues of our times, then our fundamental institutions have got to get involved. So, too, with institutions of higher education.

Our democracy—our liberty—our freedom still depend on informed citizen participation, and we presage the decline of our civilization if we think the issues are utterly beyond citizens' comprehension. We can be discouraged by the complexity of today's issues and concerned that people won't make the right decisions for themselves, their families, and their communities, but there is wisdom and comfort still in Thomas Jefferson's advice: "I know of no safe depository of the ultimate powers of society, but the people themselves; and if we think them not enlightened enough to exercise their control with a wholesome discretion, the remedy is not to take it from them, but to inform their discretion by education."

At the very least, your institutions represent a valuable resource to help articulate these issues and the options open to us. Sometimes people in the hard sciences feel that it is a waste of their time and not necessarily their responsibility to help explain these matters to laypersons. I note, though, that they are willing and surprisingly able to explain to reporters even such obscurities as DNA and nuclear fission. No part of our society can shirk a share of the responsibility for an informed electorate. It is fair to ask what your institutions are doing "to inform their discretion by education."

. . . .

To summarize, the five basic points are these:

- The United States is the longest-lived democracy in the history of the world.
- This democracy has provided almost all of us with greater freedom and opportunity than any nation of human beings has ever known.
- Among the crucial factors that foster and preserve that democracy and those freedoms are active citizenship and personal community service.
- There are clear signs that citizen participation and community service may not be as vital a part of our society for the current younger generations and those who come after them.
- No leader or leadership institution—particularly no educator or educational institution—can presume that fostering active citizenship to prolong our democracy to extend those glorious freedoms to those who come after us is someone else's business.

27
The Meaning of Volunteering

PEOPLE WHO GET involved with public causes open themselves to frustration and disappointment, but through it all and after it all, those moments of making change happen for the better are among our lasting joys. There's something wonderfully rewarding in being part of an effort that makes a difference. And there's something sparkling about being among other people when they're at their best too.

When any of us takes inventory of the meaning of our lives, these special experiences have to be among the high points. Happiness is, in the end, a simple thing. Despite how complicated we try to make it or the entrapments we substitute for it, happiness is really caring and being able to do something about it.

From *Effective Leadership in Voluntary Organizations: How to Make the Greatest Use of Citizen Service and Influence*, by Brian O'Connell. New York: Walker and Company, 1980. Copyright 1976..

In the community sense, *caring* and *service* are giving and volunteering. As far back as the twelfth century, the highest order and benefit of charity was described by Maimonides in the Mishna Torah: "The highest degree; than which there is nothing higher, is to take hold of a Jew who has been crushed and to give him a gift or a loan or to enter into partnership with him or to find work for him, and then to put him on his feet so he will not be dependent on his fellow man." That's still a very good description of empowerment.

In a world not many decades removed from the slaughter of six million Jews and still rampant with disease and other indignities of the vilest form and breadth, there is room for concern and caring, charity and volunteering. Indeed, in this still young democracy there is total dependence on citizen determination to preserve the freedoms so recently declared and to extend them to all.

The problems of contemporary society are more complex, the solutions more involved, and the satisfactions more obscure, but the basic ingredients are still the caring and the resolve to make things better. From the simplicity of these have come today's exciting efforts on behalf of humanitarian causes ranging from equality to the environment and from health to peace.

In the course of these efforts there is at work a silent cycle of cause and effect which I call the "genius of fulfillment," meaning that the harder people work for others and for the fulfillment of important social goals, the more fulfilled they are themselves. Confucius expressed it by saying that "Goodness is God," meaning that the more good we do, the happier we are, and the totality of it all is a supreme *state* of being. Thus, he said, God is not only a Supreme Being *apart* from us, but a supreme state of being *within* us.

Aristotle, too, caught an important part of it when he said, "Happiness is the utilization of one's talents along lines of excellence."

A simpler way of looking at the meaning of service is a quotation from an epitaph:

What I spent, is gone
What I kept, is lost
But what I gave to charity
Will be mine forever.

Whether we want to express the meaning of service in involved ways or prefer simpler forms doesn't really matter. It can be charity or enlightened self-interest or people's humanity to people. These are all ways of describing why we volunteer, why volunteering provides some of our happiest moments, and why the good that we do lives after us.

Index

A

ACCESS, 199
Across the Board, 122
Acts of Compassion (Wuthnow), 18
Advertising Council Public Service Award, 131
Advocacy: as function of nonprofit organizations, 42–46, 54–57; regulation of nonprofits engaged in, 73, 75, 83–84
Albrecht, Kenneth L., 125
Alcoholics Anonymous (AA), 53
Allred, Gloria, 55–56
American Bible Society, 27
American Philanthropy (Bremner), 6, 25
America's Voluntary Spirit (O'Connell), 225
Arts and humanities, giving to, 3
Association of Governing Boards of Universities and Colleges, 200
Axelrod, Nancy, "A Guide For New Trustees," 158

B

Bellah, Robert, et al, *The Good Society*, 18
Benefits, employee, in nonprofit organizations, 173, 175
Berger, Renee. *See* Knauft, E.B.
Board meetings, 162–163
The Board Member's Book (O'Connell), 138
Board of directors, 138–150; chairperson (*see* Chief volunteer officer); chief volunteer officer, 142–143; controversial issues and, 145–146, 162–163, legal responsibilities, 154–155; of national associations, 163–164; personal qualifications, 158–159; president (*see* Chief volunteer officer); responsibilities, 140–144, 154–158, 160–162, 165, 171, 174
Booth, J.D. Livingston, 4
Boudinot, Elias, 27
Bremner, Robert H., *American Philanthropy*, 6, 25
Broder, David, *Changing of the Guard*, 184
Bronk, Detlev, 80
Brown, Bertram, 188
Budgeting in nonprofit organizations, 141–142
Burke, James, 131
Bush, George, 67
Business: compared with nonprofit sector, 119–122, 157–158; competition with nonprofit organizations, 87–88
Business Roundtable, 131

C

California Heart Association, 196–197
California Lung Association, 196
Campus Outreach Opportunity League (COOL), 198
Camus, Albert, 180
Career development: in philanthropy and nonprofit sector, 195–199, 227–228; for public service, 226–227

Carnegie, Andrew, 30, 32
Carnegie Corporation of New York, The, 31, 61, 179
Carnegie Endowment for International Peace, The, 31-32
Carter, Richard, *The Gentle Legions*, 39
Case Western Reserve University, Mandel Center for Nonprofit Organizations, 198
CBS, Inc., 62
Center for Nonprofit Boards, 200
Cerebral Palsy Association of New York, 53-54
Chairperson of the board of directors. *See* Chief volunteer officer in nonprofit organizations
Changing of the Guard (Broder), 184
Chase, Irving, 189
Chavez, Cesar, 189
Chicago Community Trust, 179
Chief executive officer. *See* Chief staff officer in nonprofit organizations
Chief staff officer in nonprofit organizations, 146-148; selection of, 166-172
Chief volunteer officer in nonprofit organizations, 142-143
The Christian Century, 80
Christian College Coalition, The, 178-179
Christian Medical College Board, The, 179
Citizens' Union, The, 28
Civic and public issues, giving to, 4
Civil rights movement, 60-63
Cleveland, Harlan, 184
Cohn, Anne, 178
Combined Federal Campaign, 83
Commission on Interracial Cooperation, 60
Committee on Voluntary Action, 41
Community foundations, 35, 109, 110, 111-115; annual giving by, 109
Community Service Fellowships, 179
Compensation in nonprofit organizations. *See* salaries and compensation in nonprofit organizations
Conference of White Southerners on Race Relations, 60

Corporate foundations, 68, 127-130; 194-195; staff, 127-129; suggested initiatives for, 205-213
Corporate philanthropy, 29-30, 74, 123-132, 204; areas of interest, 124-125, 129; and public service, 123-124, 126-127, 129
Council of Better Business Bureaus, Philanthropic Advisory Service, 155
Council of Jewish Federations, 195
Curti, Merle: "American Philanthropy and the National Character," 17; "Tradition and Innovation in American Philanthropy," 81

D

Dahlberg, Jane S., *New York Bureau of Municipal Research*, 28
Davis, Michael, 141, 153
D.A.W.S. (Disabled American Workers Security), 55
Dayton, Kenneth L., 157
Democracy and volunteerism, 17-19
Dewey, John, 17
Dorsey, Eugene, 204
Drucker, Peter, 134; "What Business Can Learn From Nonprofits," 121
Duke, Lynn, "A Campaign of Civil Disobedience," 57-58
Dunbar, Lester, 62
Durfee Foundation, 179
Durham Conference, 60

E

Echohawk, John, 25, 59-60
Education: for careers in philanthropy and the nonprofit sector, 195-199, 226; giving to, 3, 26-27, 28, 30, 31, 125-126
Education Commission of the States, 198,
Eliot, Charles W., 88
Empowerment, 42-43, 57-64
The Endangered Sector (Nielsen), 9, 69-70
Equitable, 125
Escape From Freedom (Fromm) 190,

Index

Ethics of nonprofit organizations, 149–150
Evans, Eli, 61

F

Ferretti, Fred, 52
Filene, Edward A., 35
Finn, David, "Public Invisibility of Corporate Leaders," 130–131
Fleischmann, Max C., 35
Fleischmann Foundation, 35
Ford Foundation, 25, 179
The Foundation: Its Place in American Life (Keppel), 35
Foundations: giving by, 68, 109; role in society, 109; staff, 127–129; *See also* Community foundations; Corporate foundations; Corporate philanthropy; Philanthropy
Friends of Clinton Hill, 154
Fromm, Erich, *Escape From Freedom*, 190
Fundraising, 139–140, 160; regulation of, 84–85

G

Galbraith, John Kenneth, 125
Gardner, John, 7, 9, 199; *Self-Renewal*, 114
General Education Board, 36
General Electric, 125–126
General Motors, 125
The Gentle Legions (Carter), 39
Giving: to art and humanities, 3; for civic and public issues, 4; to education, 3, 26–27, 28, 30, 31; to health and hospitals, 3; by individuals, 3–4, 68, 74, 133, 216, 217–218; to international affairs and peace, 31–32; to religion, 3, 14, 27; to social welfare, 3; *See also* Corporate philanthropy; Foundations; Philanthropy
Goddard, Robert H., 23–25
Goff, Frederick, 35–36
Goldenson, Estelle, 54
Goldenson, Leonard, 54
The Good Society (Bellah et al), 18

Governing Boards (Houle), 158
Government: and regulation of nonprofit sector, 73–75, 83–88, 220–221; relationship with nonprofits in delivery of human services, 94–103; responsibility for human services, 72–76, 95–99; role of community foundations in improving, 111–112
Government funding of nonprofit sector, 46–49; and independence of organizations, 47, 88–89, 220–221
Gray, Sandra T., *See* Knauft, E.B.
Great Britain, nonprofit sector in, 72
Guggenheim, Daniel, 24
Guggenheim, Harry, 24
Guggenheim, Mrs. Harry, 24
Guggenheim Foundation, Daniel and Florence, 24
Guggenheim Memorial Foundation, John Simon, 36
Gwathmey, Bette-Ann, 53

H

Hackett, Edward. *See* Mirvis, Philip
Harriman, Mrs. E.H., 28–29
Harvard Business School/Dively Award for Corporate Public Initiative, 124
Hausman, Ethel, 53–54
Hausman, Jack, 53–54
Havel, Vaclav, 19
Head Start, 31
Health and hospitals, giving to, 3
Heiskell, Andrew, 126
Hickey, Margaret, 99
Hispanic Policy Development Project, 62
Hodgkins Fund of the Smithsonian Institution, 23
Holmes, Oliver Wendell, 32
Honeywell Inc., 126
Hoover, Herbert, 75
Houle Cyril O., *Governing Boards*, 158
House Select Committee to Investigate Foundations and Other Organizations (Reece Committee), 80
Hubert Fund, 35

Human services, nonprofit sector as providers of, 42–43, 44, 46, 73, 89, 94–103,
Hunter, David, 64

I

IBM, 124
Independent sector. *See* Nonprofit sector
INDEPENDENT SECTOR, 81, 84, 150, 180, 197, 199, 200; "Blueprint for Substantial Growth in Giving and Volunteering in America," 195; "From Belief to Commitment," 5, 14; "Giving and Volunteering in the United States," 2, 3, 4, 14, 68; "Profiles of Excellence," 212; "Research in Progress," 200; salary of chief volunteer officer, 174; "The Third Sector," 9
Indiana University, University Center on Philanthropy, 198
In-kind gifts, 29–30
Institute for Nonprofit Organization Management, 198
International affairs and peace, giving to, 31–32
Interspace, 124
Irwin, Inez Haynes, *The Last Days of the Fight for Women's Suffrage*, 11
Israel, nonprofit sector in, 82

J

Jefferson, Thomas, 7–8
Jones, Mary Harris, 59
Jones, Reginald, 131
Jordan, Vernon, 62
Jorge Prieto Humanitarian Award, 52
Joyce, James, 26

K

Keppel, Frederick P., *The Foundation: Its Place in American Life*, 35
Knauft, E.B., Renee Berger and Sandra T. Gray, *Profiles of Excellence*, 150
Kotz, Nick, 184

Kresge Foundation, 179

L

Labor Department, U.S., "America Volunteers," 39, 40
Ladies Bountiful (Rogers), 26
The Last Days of the Fight for Women's Suffrage (Irwin), 11
Law Students' Civil Rights Research Council, 61
Leadership: development of future civic, 181–186, 198–199; qualities necessary for, 185
Lear, Norman, 66
Levin, Leonard, 188
Levis, Wilson, *Taking Fund Raising Seriously*, 209
Lewis, Roger K., "Citizens Increasingly Active, Savvy in Fighting Battles with Developers," 57
Lightner, Candy, 52
Lincoln Filene Center, 198
Lindbergh, Charles, 24
Lomask, Milton, *Seed Money*, 24
Lyman, Richard W., 7

M

MADD (Mothers Against Drunk Driving), 52
Making Democracy Work (Putnam), 19
Mandel, Morton, 197–198
Mandel Center for Nonprofit Organizations, 198
Marts, Arnaud C., *Philanthropy's Role in Civilization*, 30–31
Matching gifts, 125–126
Mather, Cotton, 10
Mathews, David, 18–19
Maurice Falk Medical Fund, 180
McGuffey's Reader, 11–12
Mental Health Association, 121
Meyers, Randall, 119
Minnesota Citizens League, The, 101
Mirvis, Philip, and Edward Hackett, "Work and Work Force Characteristics in the Nonprofit Sector," 22
Moe, Henry Allen, 27, 80

Index

Montpelier Seminary, 27
Mosely, Philip E., 32
Mother Jones, 59
Moynihan, Daniel Patrick, 122
Mutual-help organizations, 3, 52–53

N

NAACP Legal Defense and Education Fund/Earl Warren Legal Training Program, 61
Nason, John W., "Trustee Responsibilities," 156
National Charities Information Bureau, 135, 155; *The Volunteer Board Member in Philanthropy*, 158–159; "What a Good Board Member Does," 158
National Court Appointed Advocate Association (CASA), 56
Native American Rights Fund, 25, 59–60
New York Bureau of Municipal Research (Dahlberg), 28
New York Times, The, "From Ashes of Tragedy, Self-Help," 52
New York Training School for Public Service, 29
Niebuhr, Rheinhold, 76
Nielsen, Waldemar, *The Endangered Sector*, 9, 69–70
9 Who Care Awards, 55
Nonprofit organizations: advocacy as function of, 42–46, 54–57, 73, 75, 83–84; board of directors, 138–152; chief staff officer, 146–148, 166–172; comparison with business, 119–122, 157–158; effectiveness of, 45–46, 120–121, 146, 147, 150–152; employee benefits, 173, 175; executive director (*see* Chief staff officer); fundraising, 84–85, 139–140, 160; sabbaticals and leaves, 177–180; salaries and compensation, 148, 173–176, 200; staff development, 194–198, 227–228; staff role, 127–129, 140–141; standards of performance, 155–156
Nonprofit sector: future of, 181–186, 216–222; government funding, 46–49, 88–89, 220–221; in Great Britain, 72; history, 37–40, 75–76; independence of, 9, 47, 75, 80–81, 83–86, 88, 89, 220–221; in Israel, 82; literature and research on, 199–200, 224–225; as providers of services, 42–43, 44, 46, 73, 89, 94–103; public attitudes toward, 90–92, 216–217; and Reagan Administration, 73–75; regulation of, 75, 83–88, 220–221; responsibilities of government vs., 72–76, 95–99; size of, 68, 71; training and education for careers in, 113–114, 195–199
Norris, Ruth, "Audubon People," 56

O

O'Connell, Brian: *America's Voluntary Spirit*, 225; *The Board Member's Book*, 138; *Philanthropy in Action*, 20, 21; Values, 177
O'Connell, Brian, and Ann O'Connell, *Volunteers in Action*, 20–21
Office of Management and Budget (OMB), 83
Office of Personnel and Management, 83

P

Packwood, Bob, 134
Parents of Murdered Children, 52
Payton, Robert L., 92; "Major Challenges to Philanthropy," 155, 224–225
Peabody, Elizabeth, 31
Pearsons, D.K., 27
People for the American Way, 66
Perpetual trusts, 33–36
Personal fulfillment through service, 187–191, 231–233
Peterson Commission Report, 104
Philanthropy, 11–12; history, 4–7 (*see also* Nonprofit sector, history); as a national characteristic, 4–7, 17–18; role of community foundation in strengthening, 112–113; training and education in, 113–114, 195–199. *See also*

Community foundations;
Corporate foundations;
Corporate philanthropy;
Foundations; Giving
Philanthropy in Action (O'Connell), 20, 21
Philanthropy's Role in Civilization (Marts), 30
Philip Bernstein Training Center, 195
Plinio, Alex, and Joanne Scanlon, *Resource Raising*, 29
Pomeroy, Florette White, 53
Pratt, Charles, 26
Pratt Institute, 26
President's Task Force on Private Initiatives, 74
Prieto, Jorge, 51
Profiles of Excellence (Knauft et al), 150
Program on Nonprofit Organizations, 198
Project Amnesty, 55–56
Project leaves in nonprofit organizations, 177–180
Public policy. *See* Advocacy; Empowerment; Government, regulation of nonprofit sector
Public Service, career development and education for, 226–227
Putnam, Robert D., *Making Democracy Work*, 19

R

Radical Principles (Walzer), 184
Reagan, Ronald, 67, 72
Reagan Administration and nonprofit sector, 73–75
Reece Committee, 80
Regulation of nonprofit organizations, 83–88, 220–221; and advocacy activities, 75, 83–84; and fundraising, 84–85
Religion and religious institutions: giving to, 3, 14, 27; role in nonprofit sector, 5–6, 13–16,
Reser, Carrie May, 55
Resource Raising (Plinio and Scanlon), 29
Reston, James, 40

Rockefeller, John D., 3rd, "America's Threatened Third Sector," 89, 119, 122
Rockefeller Brothers Fund, 35
Rogers, William G., 26
Rooks, Charles, 63
Root, Elihu, 80
Rosenwald, Julius, 33–34
Rosenwald Fund, Julius, 34–35, 60

S

Sabbaticals, 177–180
Salamon, Lester, 94, 95
Salaries and compensation in nonprofit organizations, 148, 173–176, 200
San Francisco Bay Area Business Leadership Task Force, 127
Scanlon, Joanne. *See* Plinio, Alex
Schaumberg v. Citizens for a Better Environment, 84
Seed Money (Lomask), 24
Selby, Cecily Cannan, 121
Self-Renewal (Gardner), 114
Seymour, Harold, 160
Smith, Lee, 124, 126
Social Security Act, Title XX, 46
Social welfare, giving to, 3. *See also* Human services
Society for Crippled Children and Adults, 196,
Southern Regional Council, 60–61, 62
Staff in nonprofit organizations: development, 194–198, 227–228; role, 127–129, 140–141. *See also* Chief staff officer
Stahr, Elvis, "We Must Help Each Other," 119
Stanford, Leland, 26
Stanford University, 26
"A Step Toward Equal Justice," 61–62
Stern, Edgar, 35
Stern, Edith R., 34–35
Stern, Odile, 52
Stern Fund, Edith and Edgar, 34–35

T

Taking Fund Raising Seriously (Levis), 209
Tax Act of 1986, 74
Tax policy, 73, 83–84, 87, 88; and charitable deductions, 86
Thatcher, Margaret, 72
Tocqueville, Alexis de, 6
Trustees. *See* Board of directors
Tufts University, Lincoln Filene Center, 198

U

United Cerebral Palsy, 54
U.S. Philanthropic Foundations (Weaver), 32
United Way Institute, 200
University of San Francisco, Institute for Nonprofit Management, 198
Up From Slavery (Washington), 10–11

V

Values, (O'Connell), 177
Vanderbilt University, Center for Health Services, 54
Vasconcellos, John, 183
Voluntary Organizations. *See* Nonprofit organizations
Voluntary sector. See Nonprofit sector
The Volunteer Board Member in Philanthropy, 158–159
Volunteerism, 187–191, 231–233; and corporate philanthropy, 126–127; by field of interest, 4; history, 4–7; 37–39
Volunteers, 2–3; dollar value of time contributed by, 2, 68; number of, in U.S., 2

Volunteers in Action (O'Connell and O'Connell), 20–21
Voter education, 62–63
Voter Education Project, 62–63

W

Walzer, Michael, *Radical Principals,* 184
Warner, Amos, 94
Washington, Booker T., *Up From Slavery,* 10–11
Washington Post, The, "Citizens Increasingly Active, Savvy in Fighting Battles with Developers," 57
Weaver, Warren, *U.S. Philanthropic Foundations,* 32
Weber, Joseph, "Managing the Board of Directors," 155
Westbrook, Robert, 17
Westinghouse Electric Corporation, 126
Weyerhaeuser Company, 124
Whitney, Payne, 35
Williams, Roger M., 64
Wilson, Woodrow, 18
Winthrop, John, 5
Women as volunteers, 3
Women's Foundation, 63–64
Women's rights, 11, 63–64
Wood, Dick, 26–27
Wuthnow, Robert, *Acts of Compassion,* 18

Y

Yale University, Program on Nonprofit Organizations, 198
Ylvisaker, Paul, "The Urban Issues," 109
Young, John C., 46